THE GOOD STRAIGHT ENGLISHWOMAN

THE GOOD STRAIGHT ENGLISHWOMAN

By Amanda Davies

ORFORD BOOKS

First published in Great Britain in 2005 by Orford Books

A CIP catalogue record for this title is available from the British Library.

ISBN 0 954 66531 7

Typeset in Minion and Myriad Web by Miranda Potter,
132 Blinco Grove, Cambridge, UK.

Printed and bound at the University Press, Cambridge.

Published by Orford Books, Orford, Suffolk, UK.

Contents

Illustrations

The following have kindly given me permission to reproduce illustrations:

Evelyne Diebolt: photographs on pages 99 and 101
Michael Kidd: photographs on pages 11 and 37
Lewisham Local Studies Library: photograph on page 35
Reading University Library: engraving on page 16.

Acknowledgements

I would like to thank the following people for their invaluable help in producing this book:

My aunt, Meriel Whitbread, who sent me the package from Vancouver that got me started;

Jane and Richard Balls for allowing me to write in their summer-house;

Julian Potter for his careful editing of my script and the numerous improvements he suggested, and his wife, Valerie, for her wise contributions;

Miranda Potter for her many creative ideas, including the beautiful end-papers, and her meticulous typesetting;

James Hale, literary agent and editor, who believed in this book and encouraged me to persevere with it; I am sad that he did not live to see it published;

the extraordinarily kind and patient individuals who work in the archives listed at the end of each chapter;

and the James Peek Trust for their financial support.

I am grateful to the following for permission to use material, either as a direct quotation or as a source of information:

Christopher McCall for: R. H. McCall's 1983 version of *Joseph Kidd 1824–1918* by Walter Kidd (published privately, 1920) and *When That I Was* by Dorothy McCall (Faber, 1951);

The Society of Authors as the Literary Representative of the Estate of Lady Fortescue for: *Beauty for Ashes* by Lady Fortescue (William Blackwood & Sons, 1948);

A P Watt Ltd, on behalf of The Royal Literary Fund for: *Strictly Personal* by W. Somerset Maugham (Doubleday, 1941).

For Anna, William and Harry

Preface

The last time I saw my great-aunt was on St Valentine's Day in 1978. She was a tall, slim, erect woman with piercing blue eyes and she was making her way purposefully but somewhat gingerly across the snowy lawn of the residential hotel in Surrey where she had lived for the past fifteen years. Although the sun was shining brightly, she had wrapped up well in an overcoat, scarf, gloves and fleece-lined zip-up boots. In one hand she clutched her cherrywood walking stick and in the other a brown paper bag full of crusts of bread. Clare Hedley-Peek, ninety-two years of age, was off to feed the birds. Three days later she was dead. Eight people attended her funeral.

Clare never married and she brought no children into the world. She wrote no books, painted no pictures, made no great scientific discoveries. She never had much money and certainly never sought fame or recognition of any kind. And yet throughout my childhood 'Auntie Car' was nothing short of a legend in the family, 'the sort of person someone really ought to write a book about'. Twenty-five years after her death I decided to write that book, and since then I have been on a fascinating journey of discovery. What I have uncovered is not just the story of one truly extraordinary woman, but of a whole generation of extraordinary women who saw the chief purpose of their lives as being of service to others and clearly did not see husband, hearth and home as essential to that endeavour. The years that Clare's life spanned (1885–1978) saw not only enormous industrial, sociological and scientific change, not to mention the devastation of two world wars, they also saw the most radical shift that has ever taken place in the role and position of women in society. Numerous female pioneers march through the pages of this book, both as individuals and as members of great sisterhoods. And finally my book tells the story of a remarkable friendship between Clare and her partner, Winifred Morris – a friendship that was to last for sixty-four years.

It was not long after deciding to embark on this project that I hit a serious obstacle. There was virtually no material to go on – no letters, no documents, no diaries and very few family members who remembered anything about Clare other than the odd amusing anecdote. Clare had been a faithful diary-writer all her life, but when in 1940 she had just twenty-four hours to decide which of her possessions she could carry with her on the last coal boat out of France, she went into the garden, built a bonfire and burnt every one of her diaries. As an old lady she was always reluctant to talk about her life, answering enquiries with 'Oh you don't want to hear about all that,' and as a young woman I was too preoccupied to press her for answers. How I wish now that I had. I set about putting everything that I knew – depressingly little – into chrono-logical order and then informed the few surviving members of my family who had known Clare about what I was doing. Before long a brown-paper package arrived from a niece of Clare's in Vancouver. It contained, among other things, two driving logbooks, her medals and, to my delight, her photograph album, which proved to be the richest source of information.

The photograph album, which had clearly been assembled by Clare late in her life, was in complete higgledy-piggledy order but it did have captions with place names and dates. Sometimes using a magnifying glass, sometimes easing photographs off the pages with a razor blade to see if anything was written on the back, I began to identify a sequence of landmarks in Clare's life that could be researched further with the help of various books, documents and archives. I was on my way – and I was surprised to discover how heady and exciting this was.

Over the next few months (no, I must be honest and admit that it was years – I did have a full-time job at the time) I read books, wrote letters and e-mails, visited archives, both in England and France, and met astonishingly helpful people. I became quite addicted to those exhilarating moments which I imagine every biographer experiences while on the trail of their subject and which can best be described by a variety of metaphors: when the penny drops, when the mist clears, when two ends can be tied together at last. I *thought* Clare had met Winifred Morris in the Victoria Hospital for Children in 1909, but the moment when I actually saw their names inscribed one above the other in beautiful copperplate handwriting in an enormous leather-bound nurses' register (that was only handed over to me once I'd put on a pair of white gloves) was so much more than a factual confirmation, it was downright moving.

And even more moving were the hot Provençal afternoons I spent in the kitchens of two of Clare's ex-patients, then aged 86 and 88, one of them telling me tearfully how she had learnt to walk at the age of six after three years in Clare's clinic – and how she now had countless great-grandchildren.

And of course there was that extraordinary modern aid to research, the Internet search engine. In the package from Vancouver there was one of those florist shop cards that people attach to wreaths. The writing on the card was definitely Clare's and appeared to be four lines of verse, but most of the words had been effaced – either washed away by rain or nibbled at by some small creature. Four consecutive words were, however, decipherable – 'whole world is lonely' – and I typed these into the search box. In less than three seconds a First World War poem appeared on my screen, and the little card was instantly legible; it had clearly been laid by Clare on her friend Winifred's grave. I wonder how long that little procedure would have taken before the digital revolution.

Some of the coincidences that have helped me unravel Clare's story have been just a bit too uncanny, and I have a suspicion that my investigations have been assisted in some way by Clare herself; I gather that biographers often feel like that. Why was it that the only information on the Irish potato famine that the Royal Homœopathic Society could give me led straight to a man who had written a book largely devoted to Clare's grandfather? Why was it that the bored young national serviceman who gave me directions in the Château de Vincennes military archives just happened to be a medical student with a particular interest in the treatment of wounded soldiers during the First World War and could point me to precisely the right shelf for surgical ambulances?

Because it is based on so little primary source material, I'm afraid you will find this book a bit uneven. The beginning and end of the book will read like a biography, and that is because I have been able to find out quite a lot about Clare's earlier years, and because a few people survive who remember her later years. For the middle years, when she was attached to various nursing institutions[1], I have had to rely almost entirely on bibliographical and archive research (I have listed my sources at the end

---

[1] Because Clare's life was almost entirely taken up with caring for the sick, a number of people have asked me, somewhat to my horror, whether I am a medical historian! Nothing could be further from the truth, and although I have tried my best to check the medical details I include, I must stress that the book's intention is anecdotal and impressionistic rather than scientific.

of each chapter). But if Clare seems to disappear from time to time, you can rest assured that she is definitely there – I have the photographs to prove it! It is probably true to say that Clare herself remains a somewhat shadowy figure in my book, probably because I did not wish to attribute emotions and beliefs that may not have belonged to her. However, I find the choice of material that she copied into her Commonplace Book so revealing of her character that I have included one of the quotations at the start of each chapter. In an attempt to discover what motivated Clare, I begin my book with the story of her grandfather, Joseph Kidd, who was to prove such a powerful influence in her life.

Perhaps the best answer to the question 'What inspired Clare, what gave her the strength to keep going?' lies in one of the last entries in her Commonplace Book – words of Bertrand Russell's:

> Three passions, simple but overwhelmingly strong, have governed my life: the longing for love, the search for knowledge, and an unbearable pity for the suffering of mankind.

It has been a strange business, reliving someone's life; I hope Clare will forgive me for doing that, and also for the inevitable inaccuracies. In a strange way I think a bit of me actually became Clare. I was certainly taken by surprise when a tear trickled down my cheek as I typed the words 'Three days later, at the age of ninety-two, Clare Hedley-Peek died'.

Amanda Davies
Spring 2005

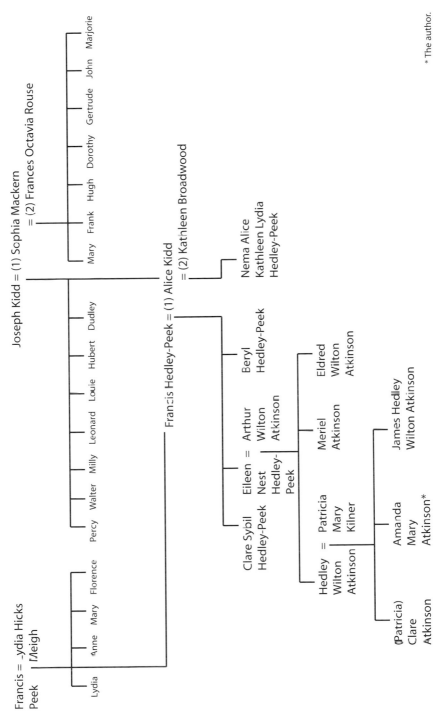

Chapter 1
Clare's Inheritance

To have no illusions, and yet to love – what stronger surety can a
woman find?

Howard's End, F. M. Forster

Clare's maternal grandfather, Joseph Kidd, was one of the most sought-
after medical practitioners of late Victorian London. He was born in
Limerick in the West of Ireland in 1824, the seventeenth of eighteen
children, and everyone knew that the little boy would be blessed with
particularly good fortune, because he was the seventh son of a seventh
son. They also knew that, in common with all seventh sons, he would
possess special healing powers. The fact that Joseph was to become
Benjamin Disraeli's medical advisor and go on to have seven sons himself
(as well as eight daughters) would seem to prove his family's predictions
to be correct.

Joseph's mother, Rebecca, came from a family of small Limerick
landowners. She had been taught when young the importance of sharing
what she had with her less fortunate neighbours and as she grew up she
found herself drawn to the Quaker tradition. Whilst she never actually
took the step of joining the Society of Friends, she nevertheless insisted
on wearing their simple dress and was much loved for her benevolence
and serenity. With her pure Celtic Irish blood, Rebecca was a great story-
teller and had a beautiful singing voice. Her marriage to Joseph's father,
who came from hardier stock, was to produce among their offspring an
interesting mix of the practical with the romantic.

Joseph's father, Thomas Keane Kidd, was descended from Cromwellian
settlers. Being very much a younger son, Thomas had no chance of following his father into the legal profession, so instead established a corn-
brokerage on a wharf near the Treaty Bridge, shipping the corn that
farmers brought him across to England or up the Shannon and via canal
to Dublin. Business flourished until a measure was introduced to assist

the West Indian sugar planters, requiring sugar rather than corn to be used in distilling both Irish and British whiskies; it soon seemed that Thomas's business was declining at about the same rate as his family was growing. The advent of the railways, together with the gradual deterioration of the Limerick harbour, dealt the final death-blow to the business some time in the 1840s.

Many of Thomas and Rebecca's children died young, and Clare's grandfather was the third son to be given the name Joseph. The family, which usually numbered about a dozen, lived in a somewhat dilapidated Georgian house on the banks of a canal leading into the Shannon, which frequently overflowed into their cellars at high tide. Sharing the house with the ever-expanding family was a succession of corn-trade apprentices, but with money becoming increasingly tight, it was made clear in their indentures that 'they must not expect salmon for dinner more than three times a week'. Although meat was not often on the menu, there was clearly a plentiful supply of butter and eggs – probably the result of some bartering between Thomas and the farmers with whom he did business – and potatoes could be bought cheaply, at six pounds for a penny.

Joseph was devoted to his mother and as a little boy he was often to be found under the table rubbing Rebecca's feet, which towards the end of her life had become painfully swollen. Before she reached the age of fifty Rebecca died, and Joseph was never to forget the sad morning when his father came into the bedroom saying 'Get up boys, you have no mother now.' From then on it fell to his eldest sister, Margaret, to bring up the family.

Joseph began his education at the local dame school, where he learnt the approved method of catching black-beetles and not much else. He went on to attend a school run by a formidable Quaker named John Tyrrel Bailey – John Terrible to his pupils – who would absent himself from the classroom at eleven o'clock each morning in order to join his wife in a dish of locally caught oysters. Joseph stayed at this school until the age of sixteen, receiving a thorough grounding in mathematics and conceiving a great love of the Classics that was to stay with him throughout his life.

As foretold, Joseph did indeed decide to enter the medical profession and without any training plunged straight from school into the emergencies of a poor country practice. One of his brothers had a dispensary at Doonas, and Joseph joined him there, helping him make up drugs and even visiting patients in his brother's absence. A year later Joseph spent six months as pupil assistant to Dr O'Shaughnessy of Limerick, continuing to dispense prescriptions but also receiving a certain amount of medical instruction. Across the road there lived another medical man whose pupil, Richard Quain, became a friend of Joseph's; the two men were to meet again more than thirty years later at Disraeli's deathbed.

At the age of eighteen Joseph went up to Dublin to become assistant to Dr William Walter of Earl Street at a salary of £25 per annum plus board and lodging. For three years he helped Dr Walter in his surgery, accompanied him on home visits and helped him in the little shop where he prepared his drugs. Although the hours were long, he was allowed two hours a day to attend lectures at the Dublin hospitals, where he learnt the anatomy, physiology, surgery and medicine that were later to earn him the diploma of the English College of Surgeons. He gained valuable experience at the Rotunda Hospital, then the most celebrated maternity hospital in Europe, and witnessed a remarkable reduction in the maternal mortality rate achieved by the simple expedient of cutting two feet off the top of the sash windows, thus increasing the ventilation.

While continuing to practise conventional medicine, Dr Walter had become extremely interested in the principles of homœopathy that had been introduced to Ireland in 1839 by Dr Charles Luther[1]. Dr Walter began tentatively to apply this new system, whereby diseases are treated with small quantities of drugs that excite symptoms similar to those of the disease itself, and Joseph shared his mentor's enthusiasm for the new method of treatment. During the last night of his time at the Rotunda, Joseph got into heated discussion on the topic of homœopathy with a couple of other students, and the following day one of them handed Joseph a copy of *The Times*, which carried an advertisement for the post of House Surgeon at the Homœopathic Hospital in London. Joseph wrote at once to the Hospital Secretary, a Mr Heurtley, who was also a senior official at the Bank of England, telling him how anxious he was to increase his knowledge of homœopathy and reassuring him that, although as yet unqualified, he felt confident that he could sit for the College of Surgeons diploma within three weeks of arriving in London. Heurtley replied that, despite Joseph's being the only unqualified applicant out of sixteen, he was 'much pleased' with his letter. This was enough for Joseph, who (with £5 in his pocket) started that night for London in order to call at the Bank of England and answer the letter in person. With the agree-

---

[1] Not a great deal is known about early homœopathy in Ireland, but it is interesting that the first English translation of the *Organon* – the primary text on the homœopathic art and science written by Samuel Hahnemann – was made by the Irishman Devrient and edited by Samuel Stratten in Dublin in 1833.

ment of the Chairman of the Hospital, Mr Sampson[1], Heurtley announced that the appointment of the House Surgeon would be postponed by a month to give Joseph a chance to sit for the diploma.

Fortunately for Joseph the diploma examinations took place more frequently then than they do nowadays, but when he went to enter his name he was disappointed to be told that there was already a full number of candidates for the next sitting. Nothing daunted, Joseph turned up on the appointed day anyway and sat in the waiting room along with the others. Just before going into the examination hall, one of the candidates got cold feet and fled from the room, whereupon Joseph sprang to his feet and took his place. Joseph passed the examination and in the summer of 1845 was offered the post of House Surgeon at the Homœopathic Hospital in Hanover Square.

Joseph quickly settled into the Homœopathic Hospital, where he was delighted to find himself working under Dr Paul François Curie[2]. Although fully committed to the practice of homœopathy, Joseph nevertheless continued his studies of orthodox or 'allopathic' medicine, as he considered it important to acquire his MD. Assuming that he could attend lectures wherever he wished as he had done in Dublin, he tried to gain access to both Guy's and King's College Hospital, only to be turned away on the grounds that he was not 'one of their students'. Refusing to accept defeat, however, he found himself a private coach and finally read for the Aberdeen MD, which he took without much difficulty. After all, why shouldn't an Irishman living in England hold a Scottish MD?

* * *

On the evening of 26th March 1847, while still working at the Homœopathic Hospital, Joseph sat down to read *The Times* and was horrified by an account of how his fellow Irishmen were suffering as a result of the potato famine that year. Before the great potato famines of 1846 and 1847, Ireland had been one of the most densely populated countries in Europe, despite having very little industry and having suffered previous localised famines. Wealthy landlords had divided up the land into small parcels, and where this was arable the crops were sold to pay the rent and usually exported to England. Most of the people lived on potatoes and buttermilk, almost without the use of money and amidst

---

[1] He was also the City correspondent of the *The Times*.
[2] Father-in-law of Marie Curie, the discoverer of radium.

a fair degree of squalor. In 1845 the potato crop failed. In 1846 and 1847 it failed again, but this time with more drastic consequences, since not only did hundreds of thousands of people die from starvation, even more perished from typhus, relapsing fever and bacillary dysentery.

This is an extract from what Joseph read that night:

> Most horrible – most dreadful are the last accounts from the west of Cork. A pestilential fever, more mortal and destructive than cholera or plague, is carrying off the poor. All the food, solid or liquid, on earth could not save them without medicinal or sanitary accompaniments of the most extensive and efficient sort. There is not a home from Bantry to Skull that, with scarce a dozen exceptions, does not contain the sick, the dying and the dead! The latter lie where they die, or are barely pushed outside the thresholds, and there suffered to dissolve. Their living relations within the huts are too feeble to remove them further; and the strong outside (and they indeed are few) are afraid to handle unshrouded and uncoffined bodies. Judge of the consequences.

This was followed by a gruesome description of how some labourers, having come across an entire family dead in their hut, were obliged to burn the place down, there being no other way to dispose of the five bodies.

It was clear that the need now was for surgeons and medical staff even more than for food. 'It flashed upon me,' Joseph was to write later, 'that there could be no more noble field in which to test the powers of homœopathy.' Joseph had read about the successful homœopathic treatment of typhus during a recent outbreak of the disease in Vienna and managed to persuade the Committee of the Homœopathic Society to call a special meeting where it was decided:

> to send at the expense of the Society Mr. Joseph Kidd, an Irishman, but a member of the London College of Surgeons – who has joyfully undertaken without the slightest prospect of reward and in the full consciousness of all the appalling circumstances with which he will be obliged to contend – to proceed to Bantry or Skibbereen, whichever should prove the most infected district, and there offer his gratuitous services and with no limit but that of the exhaustion of his own physical powers.

The choice of Bantry, Skull and Skibbereen was based on Joseph's desire to show that homœopathy could be effective in the most adverse conditions, especially where orthodox medicine had proved less than effective, but he could not possibly have known quite how adverse those conditions would be.

Hearing of the impending mission and knowing that the demand for food would be way beyond Joseph's power to satisfy, the colony of Irish Quakers who had taken Joseph to their hearts on his arrival in England immediately made a collection, to which even the youngest child contributed. On 3rd April Joseph was on his way to Cork by steamer – a voyage lasting five days. He was twenty-three years old.

Upon his arrival in Ireland Joseph decided to go first to Bantry, where he had heard the local doctor had himself fallen ill. The vicar, John Murphy, suggested that Joseph should familiarise himself with the situation immediately by accompanying him on his daily 'visit of charity', and then, writes Joseph:

> … for the first time did the full reality and extent of the desolation of the people come upon my astonished vision … I had read in English and Irish journals till the whole thing seemed a mass of exaggeration. Even so I was totally unprepared for the ghastly sights and sounds at every step. In many of the wretched huts, every inmate lay abandoned to their fate, fever and dysentery side by side on the same scanty pile of decomposing straw, or on the cold earthen floor, without food or drink.

Entering one house Joseph saw for the first time the coffins with sliding bottoms that the local people had been forced to introduce. These reusable coffins would be loaded onto carts and taken to huge pits where the bodies would be slid out. In one of these pits, before it was sealed up the following summer, lay five hundred corpses of people who had died in a single workhouse. The hospitals and other institutions were filled with the destitute, sick and dying far beyond their capacity, and the death toll from disease amongst doctors, nurses and attendants was out of all proportion to the general population.

Joseph realised that he would have to abandon any plan for a systematic operation and decided to 'devote his services promiscuously, wherever they might be needed', only taking time at night to write up his notes for the Homœopathic Society. By the end of the first week the number of cases under treatment – every one of which was carefully entered in a notebook – had grown to nearly a hundred. Just to visit half of these became a hard day's work, requiring Joseph to be out from ten in the morning until seven at night. In his later account Joseph wrote:

> The greater part of the time was spent in the most intimate contact with fever and dysentery, being frequently obliged to remain nearly half an hour in one single hovel, crowded with poor sufferers, till human nature could hold out no longer, and an instinctive and almost convulsive effort would cause me to escape from the close atmosphere of peat-smoke and fever-miasm to the open air.

How Joseph escaped infection is a complete miracle, the only precautions he took being an hour's walk every morning over the hills and 'moderation in living'.

I am certainly not competent to provide a detailed medical description of how Joseph treated his patients – in his report he lists Aconite, Bryonia, Belladonna and Nux vomica for continuing fever, Arsenicum and Phosphorus for typhus with the addition of Mercurius for dysentery. But the results he reported to the Homœopathic Society were startling; whereas the mortality rate for typhus patients in Bantry Hospital was 14%, it stood at only 1.8% among those Joseph was treating. In the case of dysentery, 13.5% of Joseph's patients died, while Bantry Hospital were losing 36% of their patients. As Joseph wrote:

> That those under homœopathic treatment, circumstanced as they were in general without proper food or drink, should have succeeded as well as the inmates of the hospital of the same town (taken from precisely the same class of people) with the advantages of proper ventilation, attendance, nourishment etc. would have been most gratifying, but that the rate of mortality under the homœopathic system should have been so decidedly in favour of our grand principle, is a circumstance, it may be hoped, which can scarcely fail to attract the attendance even of the most sceptical.

By the end of May the fever had begun to abate, and Joseph was able to turn his attention to the question of food. Semi-naked people who had barely recovered from fever were being forced to wait for up to twelve hours in the cold and wet outside hurriedly erected soup kitchens, where they would receive six ounces of food each day. Joseph contacted Mr Sampson back in London, who persuaded the British Association for the Relief of Destitution in Ireland to place a quantity of rice at Joseph's disposal. With further financial contributions, among them 100 guineas from the Archbishop of Dublin, Joseph was able to provide many hundreds with rice, bread, milk and fuel, particularly those who had recovered under his care.

The following month the Society, feeling that sufficient time had elapsed for the homœopathic trial to be considered a true one, decided to bring Joseph back to England. The level of disease was diminishing rapidly now, and a new approach to relief had been adopted under the terms of the Poor Relief (Ireland) Act of 1847, providing for the erection of sheds for those still suffering from fever and dysentery, together with additional medical care. After treating almost 200 cases, Joseph Kidd left Bantry on 15th June 1847.

The Times reported that more oats had been exported that year from Ireland than would have been sufficient to feed the whole population. Men would swim out into the Shannon to try and stop ships going down the river with oats in their holds. They were shot at in the water.

* * *

Shortly after his return from Ireland Joseph took the brave decision to resign his post at the hospital and set up as a general practitioner. With very little money in his pocket, he was fortunate to find cheap lodging with some Irish Quaker friends on Blackheath Hill, some six miles to the south-east of London, and to begin with relied on his network of faithful Quaker friends in the Peckham and Lewisham area to provide him with patients. But Joseph's reputation as a particularly sympathetic and innovative practitioner grew fast, and before long he felt able to set up an additional practice in the City of London. For just £17 a year he secured the tenancy of a consulting room and tiny waiting room on the third floor of a building in Cornhill and here spent the first two hours of each day, often walking the five miles to the City to save the nine-penny ticket for the tram from nearby Deptford. The rest of the day he devoted to those who needed attention locally – usually free of charge.

By the age of 26, and for the first time in his life, Joseph began to feel a little more financially secure. He moved into a small house in Hyde Vale, Blackheath, and his thoughts turned to the matter of finding a wife or – more specifically – to Sophia Mackern. The Mackerns were another large, rather prosperous Limerick family who lived in an impressive house named Roselawn on the banks of the River Shannon. Throughout Joseph's childhood boatloads of Kidds and Mackerns had taken to the water to fish for salmon, and two of the Mackern girls, known for their beauty as the Red Rose and White Rose of Limerick, would be invited to sing Handel arias to encourage the fish. However, it was their sister, Sophia, that Joseph remembered most tenderly, and in 1850 he invited her to join him in England and become his wife.

As Joseph became more prosperous, the young couple were able to afford to move into a larger house with a fine garden in Montpelier Row, where Percy, Walter and Milly were born. In 1859, when he was still only 35, Joseph was able to move the family once again, this time into a magnificent house named Brooklands, designed and lived in from 1825 to 1838 by one of the earliest members of the Institute of British Architects, George Smith. Brooklands stood in the most fashionable area of Blackheath and was surrounded by fourteen acres of grounds, complete with lake[1]. Here, in just eight years, five further children were added to the family: Leonard, Louie, Hubert, Dudley and lastly Alice, who was to become Clare's mother.

By now Sophia, who had suffered for most of her life from chronic bronchitis – and perhaps weakened by her repeated pregnancies – had fallen victim to severe emphysema. Tragically for Joseph, who counted himself particularly successful in the area of pulmonary disease, he was unable to save his young wife, and in 1872 she died. With eight small children to care for, Joseph sent to Limerick for his sister-in-law, the White Rose, to come and take charge of the household. Three years later Joseph was married again, this time to Frances Octavia Rouse who, at eighteen years of age, took on eight stepchildren, three of whom were older than she was. Undaunted by the task, Frances went on to have seven children of her own – Mary, Frank, Hugh, Dorothy, Gertrude, John and Marjorie – making fifteen children in all.

In the meantime Joseph's reputation was growing rapidly, and the consulting rooms in Cornhill had become quite inadequate, both in terms of the number and the status of his patients. Larger premises were found in Moorgate Street, and additional consulting rooms taken in Hanover Square to accommodate patients from the West End of London. Joseph had an idiosyncratic, not to say non-existent, appointment system,

---

[1] The land is now covered by an estate of houses known as Brooklands Park.

and on the walls of both waiting rooms there hung a notice reading:

> No appointments made; no one seen at any particular hour. Those
> who arrive late incur the risk of being too late, finding perhaps
> fifteen or twenty before them; enough to fill up the day.… Under
> any circumstance please do not return after two o'clock, as to do so
> causes much trouble and inconvenience.

He kept one lady patient waiting so long that she got hungry and
proceeded to eat Joseph's lunch, which she found on a shelf in the waiting
room. Being a man who did not waste words, he also had a notice in large
handwriting placed in a prominent position in his consulting room
containing the exhortation 'Don't talk about the weather and don't ask
how I am'.

The homœopathic system, with which Joseph was still largely identified,
enjoyed wide popularity among men and women of rank and culture at
that time. When, in 1877, Benjamin Disraeli appointed him as his medical
advisor, the majority of the Conservative cabinet followed suit, as did
several members of the peerage, including the Duke of Northumberland
and Lord Salisbury. Disraeli's diary entry for 29th September 1877 records:

> Dr. Kidd, whom all my friends wish me to consult … won't be in
> town until the middle of October, and is such a swell that, I
> believe, he only receives, and does not pay visits – convenient for
> a Prime Minister!

He did, however, succeed in seeing Joseph on 7th November and
afterwards writes:

> I entertain the highest opinion of Dr. Kidd; all the medical men I
> have known, and I have seen the highest, seem much inferior to him,
> in quickness of observation, and perception, and reasonableness,
> and at the same time originality, of his measures.

One of the more original of Joseph's measures required this particular
patient to replace his daily intake of Port with a bottle of Château Lafite.

The following summer Disraeli was taken ill at the Berlin Congress,
and Joseph was summoned by telegraph to attend to him there. He spent
several days with him until the Prime Minister was able to return to

England bearing 'peace with honour'. Joseph did not accept the Prime Minister's invitation to return with him in state; he had by now become a member of the Plymouth Brethren and, being forbidden to appear in public, he preferred to come home quietly and alone. In 1881 Disraeli's life was drawing to its close, and Queen Victoria ordered that her Prime

Joseph Kidd aged 92

Minister be attended by an allopathic doctor in addition to Dr Kidd. The eminent doctor Sir Richard Quain was summoned, and so the two old friends from the back streets of Limerick found themselves standing on either side of the death-bed. Disraeli died with his left hand in Joseph's.

In terms of religious affiliation Joseph remained essentially a nonconformist. With his Quaker-style background he preferred to worship at first in the Congregational and English Presbyterian churches in South East London until eventually becoming a member of the Plymouth Brethren at the age of forty-two. He took a special interest in the Bible Society, the London City Mission founded by his friend Charles Spurgeon, the Church Missionary Society, the Salvation Army and the movement known as the Factory Girls of the Isle of Dogs. Patients from the evangelical circles in which Joseph moved became regular visitors to Brooklands, including the great Victorian philanthropist George Peabody and the founders of the Salvation Army, William and Catherine Booth. But his success in the wide circle of the great and the good never diminished Joseph's concern for those he described as 'poor in this world's goods'. When an elderly governess, whose health had been broken down by years of toil, came to his consulting rooms, Joseph gave her a thorough examination and then told her that he would send her prescription later that day. The 'prescription' that arrived that afternoon was a cheque for £100 with accompanying instructions, 'This is to pay for you to have a long holiday by the sea'.

On the last page of his book *The Laws of Therapeutics*, which he dedicated 'To the Advancement and Diffusion of Truth', Joseph wrote:

I search out for myself what I desire to make known to others – every aid for the sick and suffering that science and art can give the physician, taking at their true value all laws and principles of healing, and using them for the elaboration and perfecting of the art of medicine; so that I may be a workman approved of my Master, and a servant fit to minister amongst the sick, the sorrowful and the weak.

There could be no more fitting epitaph for his granddaughter, Clare.

Sources

Bantry Library, Ireland.

British Homœopathic Association Library, London.

British Library – Newspaper Library, Colindale.

Kidd, Joseph. Homœopathy in acute diseases: narrative of a mission to Ireland during the famine and pestilence of 1847. In *Truths and their reception considered in relation to the doctrine of homœopathy*, Sampson, Marmaduke B., pp. 202–251. Samuel Highley, for the British Homœopathic Association, 1849.

Kidd, Joseph. *The Laws of Therapeutics*. C. Keegan Paul, 1881.

Kidd, Walter. *Joseph Kidd 1824–1918, Limerick London Blackheath; a Memoir*. Published privately, 1920.

McCall, Dorothy. *When That I Was*. Faber & Faber, 1952.

Treuherz, Francis. *Homœopathy in the Irish Potato Famine*. Samuel Press, 1995.

Chapter 2
Tea and Biscuits

Money … is none of the wheels of trade: it is the oil which renders
the motion of the wheels more smooth and easy.
Essays, Moral and Political, David Hume

While one of Clare's grandfathers was building up his medical practice
among the rich, the powerful and those 'poor in this world's goods', her
other grandfather, Francis Peek, was busy running one of the top
wholesale tea brokers and dealers in the country. Joseph Kidd, who had
never cared for wealth itself, was doing his best to persuade his sons to
avoid a life of business and urging his children to look on the medical
profession as the best in the world (with apparent success, since four of
his sons and one daughter were to become doctors). Various members of
the Peek family, on the other hand, had been in the tea trade since the
beginning of the century and regarded it as a fine occupation for a
gentleman.

The Peek family had lived scattered all over Devon since the first half
of the fourteenth century, when the original Norman name, de Lucie, had
been anglicised to create first Pyke (*lucius* being the Latin for that particular
fish) and finally Peek. In about 1800 Francis's great-uncle Richard, who
was eighteen years old at the time, decided it was time to leave the remote
Devonshire village of Loddiswell and seek his fortune. After working
briefly in Kingsbridge and Plymouth, he set off to walk to London, something not uncommon among unattached young men in those days.
Crossing London Bridge on the last leg of his journey, he had the immense
good fortune to meet a Quaker gentleman whom he had known in
Devon and who was kind enough to steer him towards a job with the tea
firm of Sanderson & Barclay in Old Jewry. After seven years Richard was
promoted to the post of 'traveller' and arranged for his place in the
Sanderson & Barclay warehouse to be offered to his sixteen-year-old
brother, William, who was also keen to come to London.

After three years of working for Sanderson & Barclay, William decided to launch out on his own as W. Peek & Co. and persuaded his elder brother, Richard, to join him. The firm of Peek Brothers & Co. was born. Richard left the partnership in 1832, having been elected High Sheriff of

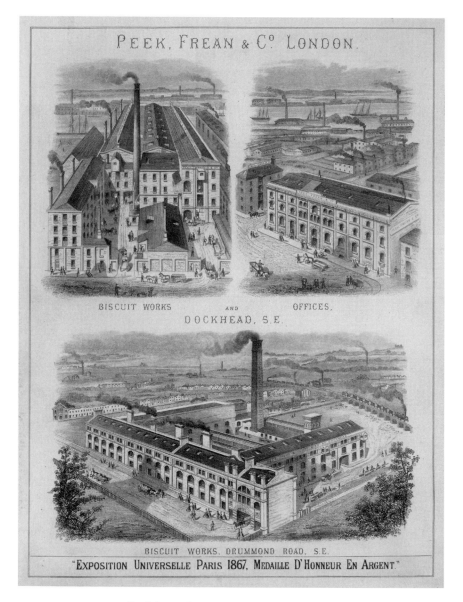

Peek Frean factory, Bermondsey, in 1867

London and Middlesex, but further members of the family continued to join the firm, including William's son, Francis. The company was expanding fast now, and by 1865 they were paying duty on over five million pounds of tea. In 1876 Francis's only son, Francis Hedley, who was to become Clare's father, joined his father in the thriving family firm.

Over the years various splits and mergers took place. At one point, two new companies were created in London and Liverpool operating in direct competition to one another, but in May 1895 it was decided to bring the three firms together under the name of Peek Brothers & Winch Ltd. It was said at the time that this would make the new company, which had agencies in China, Europe, the USA and Canada, the largest wholesale dealer of tea and coffee in the world. Clare's grandfather, Francis, was the first Chairman of the new company, and her father, Francis Hedley, also joined the Board.

Peek Brothers & Co. had had their offices at No. 20 Eastcheap in the City of London since 1842, but when Peek Brothers & Winch was created it was thought fitting that the front of the building be refurbished to reflect the expanded firm's greater confidence and market position. The name 'Peek House' was now carved in the stonework above the door, as was a fine frieze of camels laden with bales of tea being led across the desert. Underneath all this there appeared the family motto, 'le maître vient'[1] – a play on the maiden name of one of Francis's ancestors, Elizabeth Lemaître, who had fled France after the revocation of the Edict of Nantes.

Another great-uncle who had helped to establish Peek Brothers & Co. in the early years was James Peek, and this gentleman had high hopes that his two sons, Charles and Edward, aged seventeen and sixteen respectively, would follow him into the family firm as Francis had followed William. When they declared that they had no interest in tea, James decided to set them up instead in a business of their own and invited a West Country miller and ships' biscuit maker, George Hender Frean, who had married his niece, to come up to London and start a biscuit factory for his sons to run. A bakery was established in Mill Street, Dockhead on the south bank of the River Thames.

From the start nothing went right with the business, and it was not long before the brothers decided that they had no more liking for the biscuit industry than they had for the tea trade. Charles returned to Devon

---

[1] The master is coming. This may still be seen today at No. 20 Eastcheap in the City of London.

Clare's father, Francis Hedley-Peek

where he died shortly afterwards, and Edward decided that he was better suited to Holy Orders than to making biscuits. By 1857 their father found himself running the business himself, with his friend George Frean as his managing partner, and so the first mass-producer of biscuits, Peek Frean & Company, was born. It was to remain a household name for the next 130 years[1].

---

[1] In 1921 Peek Frean & Co. merged with Huntley & Palmers to create Associated Biscuits. In 1982 AB was bought by Nabisco but sold again to Danone in 1989 with the new name Jacob's Bakery Ltd.

Under James Peek and George Frean the firm at last began to prosper. By 1860 it was clear that further technical assistance was required, so Frean wrote to an old school-friend, John Carr, and invited him to join them. Carr had served an apprenticeship in his brother's biscuit factory in the North but, having fallen out with the family firm, was happy to accept the offer. The engagement of Jonathan Carr turned out to be most fortuitous for the company and might never have taken place if James had had his way; he had a deep hatred of beards which, he said, gave men an appearance 'little removed from that of a murderer or cut-throat', and Carr sported a beard of the most luxuriant variety.

Commercially produced biscuits in those days were rock-hard and not very digestible. Carr was able to develop the technology that did away with the need for the tiny 'docker-holes' that perforated the biscuits and made them so unappetizing and created a new type of biscuit, known as the Pearl, which was the forerunner of the modern biscuit. In 1866 machinery was introduced, forcing the company to move to larger premises, and this time they established their factory in an area of market gardens in Bermondsey, where they were to become a major employer in the area. The outbreak of the Franco-Prussian war in 1870, when 10 million biscuits were ordered by the Royal Navy, sealed their fortune, as did the invention of popular biscuits such as the Garibaldi, Bourbon and Shortcake[1].

In 1901 Peek Frean & Co. became a limited company, with Clare's father, Francis, (who had by now acquired the double-barrelled surname, Hedley-Peek) as its first Chairman.

Sources

The Pumphouse Educational Museum, Rotherhithe.

FINCH, Francis. *Peek of Hazelwood*, (printed privately), 1964.

FORREST Denys. *Tea for the British*, Chatto & Windus, 1973.

---

[1] The Pumphouse Educational Museum in Rotherhithe has a permanent exhibition of photographs, documents and artefacts from Peek Frean & Co.'s Bermondsey biscuit and cake factory. The Company made a six-foot cake for the wedding of Queen Elizabeth II, a replica of which is also on display in the Museum.

Chapter 3
Halcyon Childhood

It is perhaps because I know what England can mean to a thankful child that I find completely intolerable the thought of what it means to too many children, whose later memories, unlike mine, cannot rest secure between sea and meadow, the blue, the green.

Civil Journey, Storm Jameson

At her first grown-up party, Alice Kidd – Joseph's eighth child and Clare's mother-to-be – was asked 'And what, dear Alice, is to be your chosen path in life?', to which she replied brightly 'Oh I'm going to be married,'

Clare's mother, Alice Kidd

and that is precisely what she did, having chosen her partner before leaving school. The offices of Peek Brothers & Co. were a stone's throw away from Joseph Kidd's consulting rooms in the City of London, and it is very possible that Francis Hedley-Peek had reason to consult the eminent doctor, his visit perhaps resulting in an invitation to Brooklands. However the introduction came about, the couple were married in 1884 when Alice was just seventeen and Francis twenty-six.

Having joined the thriving family firm of Peek Brothers & Co. some ten years earlier, Francis was able to install his new bride in a very fine house at 3 Stanhope Terrace, just across the Bayswater Road from Hyde Park. Within a year, on 27th November 1885, Clare Sybil was born. Curiously, Francis did not register the baby's birth until the following February, although there are no records to suggest that she was anything other than hale and hearty. Perhaps her father had intended her to be a boy, in which case he was to suffer three further disappointments, leaving behind no male heir. Less than two years later Eileen Nest arrived. The two girls were inseparable from the start, Clare making a brave attempt at Eileen's name with 'Ei-Ei,' and Eileen managing just 'Car,' the names they called each other for the rest of their lives.

Life at Stanhope Terrace was extremely comfortable, with plenty of staff to ensure that it was so, but Alice, who was given to periods of melancholy, soon began to miss the fresh air of Blackheath and the vast garden of Brooklands. Francis himself was a keen huntsman, and so it was decided that the family should move away from London to the little village of Outwood in Surrey – fine hunting country and sufficiently close to London for Francis to put in a brief appearance in the City each day.

In an article he wrote for the Badminton Magazine in 1896, Francis describes Outwood as 'situated in a small, fairly level plateau covering about two hundred square miles, which considering its size, is perhaps as suitable for hunting as any in the South of England.' Francis gives his article the title *Five Miles from Anywhere*, and it is true to say that at the beginning of the 19th century, the area around Outwood was known as one of the most isolated and inaccessible places in the South of England. 'The traveller could not reach it by road,' continues Francis, 'for the place was divided from the rest of the world on every side by at least four miles of green lanes.' It was not until the construction of the Reigate to Tonbridge railway in the mid-nineteenth century that wealthy families such as the Peeks started moving into the village, either building new houses or extending existing properties. By the time the 1891 census was taken, the

Clare aged 5 and Eileen aged 3

population of Outwood had reached almost 500. In addition to the fine old post-mill, built in 1665 around the trunk of a magnificent oak tree, and the even more ancient Bell Inn, the village now boasted a church, a school, a telegraph office and a brand new road leading to it.

As a result of the settlement of Outwood by the gentry, a fine line of large houses had sprung up running from East to West through the parish, and it was into one of these that Francis moved his wife and two small daughters in 1889. Shepherds Hurst, as the house was named, had been built on land belonging to Shepherds Farm, a late 17th century farmhouse, which now stood on Francis's land and was renamed by him Shepherds Lodge. Another property that stood on the estate was the curiously named Slab Castle, which was used to house the family's coachman groom, Frederick Dean, and his wife Caroline. Other members of the household recorded in the 1891 census were a governess, Nellie Gibbs aged 17, a cook, Maud Goswell aged 18, and two servants, Sarah Larken aged 24 and Ellen Peare aged 17.

Shortly after the move into Shepherds Hurst, Francis noticed that there were five distinct ponds around the old farmhouse, three of them almost completely filled in, which he gave instructions to have dug out to their original depth. Instead of being five feet deep as expected, the ponds were found to be between fourteen and sixteen feet deep with stone paving at the bottom. It was known that there had been a religious community in the area several centuries earlier, and Francis concluded that the ponds had been dug by the monks to supply them with fish, the paving being laid to prevent the fish from having a muddy flavour. From 1771 Shepherds Farm had been used as a secret meeting place by the Baptists, who had been active in Outwood since the late 1600s, and it was known that one of the ponds had been used as a dipping place for the converts.

Shepherds Hurst itself was a large many-gabled house, facing due south at the end of a sweeping drive not far from the original farm and stables. The tile-hung front of the house soon became covered with a riot of virginia creeper, wisteria and roses so that some of the leaded windows could only be opened with difficulty. Lawns stretched away on three sides

Shepherds Hurst, Outwood, Surrey

of the house, one leading down to a small lake, and another carefully levelled to create a croquet lawn. In the stables, under the watchful eye of Frederick, were kept a fine hunter for Francis, a beautiful Irish Thorough-bred for Alice, who was a passionate and intrepid rider, and two Shetland Ponies, one for Clare called Microbe and one for Eileen called Merrylegs MacJones. As well as looking after the family's horses and ponies, Frederick was responsible for the upkeep of the diligence that took Francis to Horley station where he caught the train to Cannon Street, and the victoria in which Alice would go calling on summer afternoons. He also maintained and drove the landau that was used for family expeditions.

Childhood at Shepherds Hurst was nothing short of idyllic for Clare and Eileen, who wanted no other companion but one another. As soon as they were excused from their lessons, they would change their clothes and rush out into the garden or down to the farm, where there was plenty of fun to be had among the haystacks or collecting eggs for Ellen, the farmer's wife. Almost every day Frederick would be asked to saddle up Microbe and Merrylegs MacJones, and the girls would ride round and round the garden and finally through the back door into the kitchen, where the ponies would be given a reward for their patience. When Clare was ten and Eileen eight a new source of entertainment came into their lives with the birth of a little sister, Beryl.

The lake at the bottom of the garden was to provide endless enter-tainment, and fishing became a favourite pastime, despite the fact that the girls rarely caught anything more than minnows. Many happy hours were spent playing pirates on the island in the middle, which could be reached by means of a coracle-shaped rowing boat that had a tiresome habit of going round and round in circles. In this lake too they were given their first swimming lessons by Captain Robert Scott, who was a frequent visitor to Shepherds Hurst before he set out on his first Antarctic expedition in 1901.

Croquet was taken very seriously indeed and became a lifelong passion of Clare's[1]. Another great passion was cricket, played by girls as well as boys in those days. A lively cricket club had existed in Outwood since

---

[1] One of her nephews can remember playing with Clare when he was a small boy and she about fifty. Not satisfied with the position of his ball after taking a shot at the hoop, young Eldred, not realising that he was being watched by his eagle-eyed aunt, eased it gently sideways with his foot. Without in the least scolding her nephew, Clare declared the game over, returned her mallet to its box and left the lawn. Croquet was for her not a game to be trifled with.

1887, but in 1897 Clare's father made land available for a second club – The Shepherds Farm Cricket Club – which appeared to consist mainly of members of the church choir, who had previously been obliged to use a rough corner of the Common to play their matches. A local newspaper

Clare and Eileen at Shepherds Hurst

report describes the Shepherds Farm CC as 'a ground which, for its size, beauty and condition would excite the envy of many a more ambitious club,' and records matches against Bletchingley Hornets, The Prince of Wales XI and J. Heyman's XI. Cricket became and remained one of the high points of the summer for Clare, and she often watched matches on her very own home ground[1].

Summer holidays would be spent at Seaview on the Isle of Wight, the island having been made fashionable by Victoria and Albert's purchase and development of Osborne House[2] some decades earlier. Francis had bought one of the newly built redbrick houses with balconies and verandahs overlooking the Solent, and the family would decamp there, along with the necessary staff, every August. Another annual treat was a trip to the winter quarters of Lord John Sanger's circus at nearby Burstow Lodge. As well as watching the troup running through their acts in a practice ring, the girls were allowed to visit the four elephants, known as the 'Cruet Set' (Salt, Pepper, Mustard and Sauce), who were housed in an enormous barn constructed with timber salvaged from the old grandstand at Epsom Downs racecourse.

In their earlier years Clare and Eileen were given tuition by their seventeen-year-old governess Nellie Gibbs, known to the girls affectionately as 'Diddy'[3]. But lessons of far greater interest, valuable lessons of the countryside, were also learnt at Shepherds Hurst. Francis owned a rare breed of pigeons and had tried everything he could think of to keep the owls out of his pigeon-loft. The owls had made their nest nearby in an old cottage where bacon was cured and would make nightly excursions to the pigeon-loft to bring back baby pigeons to feed their own offspring. Finally Francis lost patience and managed to evict the owl family, only to find some weeks later that the hams, which should have weighed 10lbs once cured, weighed less than two. A small round hole was noticed in the skin of each ham, and it became clear that everything edible inside had been eaten by bats, who had then made their home in the empty shells. 'You see,' said Francis to his children 'if you kill the owls, the bats, mice and birds will soon teach you the folly of turning out your policemen.'

---

[1] In her eighties and nineties she was to become an ardent supporter of the Haslemere Cricket Club in Surrey.

[2] The Queen was to die at Osborne in January 1901. Clare's photograph collection includes a picture taken from the beach at East Cowes as the Queen's body was borne to the mainland on the Royal Yacht Alberta. It is reproduced at the end of this chapter.

[3] with whom Clare kept in touch until her death in 1940.

* * *

But only too soon, Francis and Alice had to concede that it was time for Clare and Eileen to leave childhood behind and be transformed into the young ladies that the Edwardian era required them to be. The girls were sent off to Effingham House at Bexhill-on-Sea, one of several boarding schools that had been attracted to the Sussex town by its health-enhancing reputation. Here they received tuition in Latin, French, English literature, mathematics and some rudimentary science. They were also taught drama and deportment, and Eileen was given private violin lessons, where she excelled to such a degree that she was eventually to become a violin teacher herself. In the interests of health, there were bracing walks along the beach with their form mistress and a good deal of sport was played, Clare captaining the First Cricket XI and Eileen the school tennis team. Although cricket was not uncommon at girls' schools, it did have its complications in terms of dress. The skirts the girls were obliged to wear in order to move freely unfortunately afforded a glimpse of their ankles, which was not a problem until there were 'away' matches; then the team would travel in their full-length skirts and carry their cricket skirts in a bag.

The older girls would occasionally be allowed to go into the town, as always escorted by a mistress. They would either walk in pairs along the fashionable Bicycle Boulevard or attend a concert in the Kursaal, a pavilion

Clare, classmates and mistress on Bexhill beach

built for refined entertainment and relaxation by the 8th Earl De La Warr, who was a resident of the town. In May 1902 the Earl persuaded the Automobile Club of Great Britain and Ireland[1] to help him organise the very first automobile racing event on British soil. Thousands of spectators flocked to Bexhill to witness the spectacle of motor cars racing up and down the Boulevard at speeds in excess of 50 mph (when the speed limit of the day was a mere 12 mph), and for this special occasion every girl in the school was given permission to attend. Maybe Clare never quite forgot the smell of paraffin that filled the air that day and the sound of so many throbbing, puffing and snorting motors, for driving was later to become her passion.

Much as they loved Effingham House, Clare and Eileen longed to return to Shepherds Hurst during the school holidays so that they could ride once more. By now Francis had replaced the girls' Shetland ponies with horses of a more suitable size, which contrary to custom he insisted his daughters ride astride rather than sidesaddle. Alice had recently had a serious hunting accident while riding sidesaddle; the horse she was riding had taken a fence far higher than was necessary, and Alice had been knocked out of her saddle by an overhanging branch. One of Alice's feet remained caught in the stirrup, and she was dragged for a considerable distance with the horse kicking her repeatedly in the face. Her jaw was broken in several places but was wired up in the most ingenious way, requiring her to sit for many hours a day with a clay pipe in her mouth filled with lead to ensure that the resulting new jaw was not crooked.

* * *

And what of Clare's father? Francis was clearly a most effective businessman, becoming Chairman of both Peek Bros & Winch and Peek Frean & Co., and yet by the 1891 census he was giving his profession as 'Writer'. For some time he had been deeply involved in Spiritualism, a belief system which holds that man's spirit, having survived physical death and entered the spirit world, surrounds and interpenetrates our material life. Under the right conditions, Spiritualists believe, communication of various sorts can take place between the worlds of spirit and earthly beings, this being made possible by people with mediumistic abilities. Francis wrote several lengthy books of short stories and poetry, all extraordinarily melodramatic and

[1] Subsequently the Royal Automobile Club.

turgid, and almost devoid of literary merit by today's standards. One of them, entitled *Nema* (Amen written backwards), describes various phenomena from the spirit world and has distinctly sexual undertones. His books make it clear that Francis engaged regularly in private séances.

Family lore does not reveal the extent to which Alice herself became involved in this exploration of the spirit world. It is of course true to say that the basic tenet of Spiritualism – that the soul survives physical death – is not in itself at odds with Christianity, but how Alice was able to reconcile some of her husband's more bizarre practices with her Quaker upbringing is difficult to imagine. One can only hope and assume that the children were not invited to join séances or attend the ouija table.

Not much is known about Alice, although it is certain that Clare remained extremely close to her mother right up to and beyond her death – a death which was to come tragically early. She kept a Commonplace Book[1] with many grandiose and pious entries, typical of the late-Victorian era and all tinged with sadness. Alice had been diagnosed with pulmonary tuberculosis at the age of only twenty-nine and at the age of thirty-three she died. Without having experienced such a tragedy, it is hard to imagine the impact of a mother's death on her children, but one can imagine that Clare, at the age of fifteen, must have felt the need to be especially strong for her two younger sisters, particularly little Beryl, who was barely five years old.

A year or so after Alice's death Francis decided it would be right to marry again, not least in order to provide his three girls with a mother. His choice this time fell on Kathleen Broadwood, a member of the famous piano-manufacturing family that lived not far away on their large estate, Cottesmore Hall in Pease Pottage, Sussex. Kathleen had already received a proposal of marriage from the then penniless Captain Scott but she had turned him down in favour of Francis, who, at forty-three, was some twenty years her senior. Kathleen was beautiful and lively and bred Pekinese dogs and within two years of the marriage she presented Francis with another daughter, Nema Alice Kathleen Lydia, known as Lydia. And so Francis, who had grown up with four sisters and no brothers, had four daughters and no sons himself.

But tragedy was to strike the Peek family a second time. Before Lydia was one year old Francis suffered an attack of appendicitis which was diagnosed too late and he died of peritonitis. At the age of twenty-seven

---

[1] The same book in which Clare was to write after her mother's death.

and with a new baby to care for, Kathleen found herself quite unable to cope with her three step-daughters, the eldest of whom was only eight years younger than herself, and fled back into the bosom of the Broadwood family. Clare, Eileen and Beryl were effectively orphans.

Sources
Outwood Historical Society.

JOHNSON, Michael (ed.). *A History of Outwood*, vol. 1. Outwood Local History Society, 1997.

Ibid. A History of Outwood, vol. 2. Outwood Local History Society, 1998.

National Archives, 1891 Census for Outwood, Surrey.

HEDLEY-PEEK, Francis. *Five Miles from Anywhere*, Badminton Magazine, vol. 1 no. 5, 1896.

Chapter 4
New Life in Blackheath

Illumination is not to be sought in abandonment of the world, or in ascetic practices, or in a life of abnegation and obedience, but in doing as well as we can the duties and calls of every day.
A Pilgrim's Search for the Divine, Lord Allington

The response of the Kidd family to the tragic situation was swift and undramatic; Clare, Eileen and Beryl would each be taken in by one of Alice's brothers and sisters, most of whom were still living in or around Blackheath. When Alice married Francis, she already had seven full and five half siblings, and three more had been added later. Some were about the same age or even younger than their three orphaned nieces.

Throughout her childhood, Clare's mother, Alice, had been particularly close to her older sister, Louie (always known as Loo), and had asked her to be Clare's godmother. In the circumstances it seemed natural that Loo should offer Clare a home, while Eileen and Beryl would be taken in by other members of the Kidd family. All seemed to have been satisfactorily settled, but nobody had counted on Eileen's reaction to being separated from her beloved sister, Car. When Loo saw Eileen's distress, she did not hesitate in offering a home to both the girls; the call of duty clearly did not require her to take on five-year-old Beryl, who was offered a home by another of her mother's sisters, known for some reason as Auntie Tooky. Loo had only one child, a daughter named Noel, and her husband, who had come from a large Irish family, was happy to add two more women to his household. Noel was of course delighted to acquire two new sisters, and she and Clare, being close in age, became instant and lifelong friends.

Clare and Eileen were extremely fortunate in their new home. Aunt Loo was a real live-wire with a strong republican streak to her (although when pressed, she did admit to having hung bunting outside the house when Queen Victoria made her way up Shooter's Hill Road after visiting

Boer War casualties in the Herbert Hospital.) Her husband, Jack Mackern, was the son of Sophia Kidd's brother, George, and therefore Loo's first cousin. George had been so badly behaved in Limerick that he had been shipped off to the Argentine along with his brother, Hector, who was equally badly behaved. The two brothers flourished and remained in the Argentine, Hector finishing his days smoking and playing chess in the cafés of Buenos Aires, and George flying kites[1]. George had made frequent visits home and finally decided to send his son, Jack, back to England to study at St Bartholomew's medical school alongside his cousin, Percy Kidd. Jack was extremely handsome and had inherited his father's native Irish charm, overlaying it with the Spanish manners he had acquired in the Argentine. Loo had fallen in love with Jack instantly, and they married, much to the delight of the younger Kidd children who also adored him, largely because he would spend hours making whistles for them or teaching them to make an ear-splitting noise on a blade of grass. He had inherited his father's kite-flying skill, and Kidd kites were soon flying higher than anyone else's over Blackheath.

By the time Clare and Eileen moved into the Mackern home, Uncle Jack was working as a general practitioner in partnership with another of Joseph's sons, Walter, in Shooters Hill Road, Blackheath. Joseph's eldest son, Percy, lived nearby and was working as a chest specialist in London[2], and another son, Leonard, was specialising in the nervous system up in Hampstead. In Joseph's 'second family' there were two further doctors. Mary, who was only eight years older than Clare but was nevertheless her aunt, had just completed her training at the Royal Free Hospital, the only hospital in London to offer facilities for clinical instruction to women[3]. And lastly there was Frank, who was to become an eminent surgeon of international reputation but sadly died in middle age. When one adds to this medical roll-call Joseph himself, who did not retire from practice until his ninetieth year, Clare found herself surrounded by doctors.

* * *

---

[1] An Argentinian passion to this day.
[2] He was made Fellow of the Royal College of Physicians in his late eighties and is credited by some as being one of the three men who made the Brompton Chest Hospital the pre-eminent institution it is today.
[3] She went on to work for many years as a public health doctor in maternity and child welfare clinics, writing several books on the subject.

A Deptford street

The area in which Clare was now living, and from which Uncle Jack drew his patients, was one of enormous contrasts in terms of poverty and affluence, which in some cases existed virtually side by side. To the north of the borough lay Deptford, Greenwich and Charlton, and to the south Lewisham, Blackheath and Kidbrooke. Two of those areas, Deptford and Blackheath, lying just a couple of miles apart on either side of Greenwich Park, may serve to illustrate this contrast.

Deptford, which often went by the name of Darkest Deptford or Dreary Deptford, covered an area of 1563 acres, nearly a fifth of which had been carved up by railway tracks. This left strips of land which were cut off from public use and, being unsuitable for housing, had become dumping grounds for rubbish, as well as breeding grounds for rodents. Its population density was considerably higher than many neighbouring boroughs, standing at 72 persons per acre against Lewisham's 24.8. In 1910 Deptford was the only borough in London where the death rate was higher than that of the previous year, and the infant mortality rate had risen to 189 per thousand in the eastern ward of the borough. Behind all these statistics lay low wages, intermittent employment, large families

35

and unsanitary dwellings. The average number of children in a family was five, and often their one-roomed home doubled as living room and bedroom, with the whole family sleeping in one bed. But all was not unremitting grimness and gloom in these terrible slums, and the residents of Deptford seemed determined to find some joy in the otherwise miserable conditions. There were weddings and funerals, occasional outings to Greenwich Park and steamboat rides on the river, plays in the open air and cockfights in the back yards. A survey of the area at the time commented:

> Courage and gaiety survive in the mean streets in spite of poverty, insecurity and neglect; the constant greatness of the human spirit, which refuses to be defeated by life, is not quenched in them.

Meanwhile, on the other side of Greenwich Park stood the elegant mansions of Blackheath and the lively shops and businesses that thrived in Tranquil Vale. Situated high above the smoke of London, businessmen from the City had long since adopted it as an ideal location to establish their families, with a fast rail service up to London and healthy air for their children to grow up in. There was plenty of available land for large gardens, stabling for their horses and carriages and cottages for their staff, and the heath itself offered additional space to fly kites, sail boats on the boating pond and stage hockey matches between the large families that lived dotted around. The Blackheath Conservatoire and the Literary Institute provided the culture they needed, as did a well-stocked public library, and there were a number of private day-schools to cope with the earlier education of their children before they were sent off to boarding school. This, of course, was the privileged world that Clare now inhabited.

* * *

Clare and her sisters were already familiar with their vast family of aunts, uncles and cousins. They were devoted to their step-grandmother, Frances, whom they called Aunt Fanny, but somewhat in awe of their grandfather with his high forehead, piercing eyes and flowing white beard. They knew Brooklands well, having made the relatively short journey from Outwood to Blackheath frequently throughout their childhood and always for the hay party which was still the high point of the year. Every June three old men would walk up to Blackheath from Kent with their scythes over their shoulders and mow several neighbouring meadows in turn. As each field was cut a party would be held, involving various friends and relations building hay fortresses that had to be defended and besieged, the idea being that these mad antics would help the hay to dry. This was followed by a sumptuous strawberry tea and a ride on the swings and seesaw, the latter known for some reason as the 'hystertyster', and finally a row on the lake with compulsory capsizing and mock drownings. Aunt Fanny always kept an odd assortment of spare garments for the shipwrecked to change into.

After the relatively quiet existence that Clare and her sisters had led at Outwood, they now found themselves propelled into a world that was full of ideals, projects and above all people from every possible background. Fired with Octavia Hill's magnificent vision of a 'green belt' around London, Aunt Fanny constantly threw open the grounds of Brooklands to people for whom a garden was a very rare and refreshing treat. Sunday-schools, mothers' meetings, posses of factory girls, policemen of the 'R' division, even labourers engaged in the building of the South

Mary Kidd boating on Brooklands lake

Eastern Railway 'loopline' nearby trooped up the drive to Brooklands to be given tea and cakes and a chance to go boating. After years spent in tropical climates or treeless plains, many a weary missionary feasted his eyes on the glorious flowering trees of Brooklands, while their children raced around the garden in the autumn months in search of conkers. More than one anaemic girl assured Joseph that she had never before seen trees growing, and most of the visitors went away armed with milk from Brooklands cows, fruit from Brooklands trees and very often bunches of flowers.

One of the more unusual of Fanny's Open Days was for the crew that had arrived from Japan to take over a couple of ships that had been built for them on Thamesside. While waiting to set sail, they had been spending their time wandering despondently around the docklands of the East End and, since they spoke no English, not receiving too warm a reception. A retired missionary who had spent many years in Japan came across the unhappy group of men and, having heard of Brooklands, persuaded Fanny to invite them to her home. Joseph was prevailed upon to hire a marquee for the occasion, as the missionary was adamant that the men would need to take their tea in complete privacy. The party was a huge success, and a couple of the sailors, who were Christian and who spoke English, produced a Japanese translation of a popular hymn for the sailors to sing after tea, which they agreed to do so long as they could sing their own Japanese war-song afterwards.

On the more seriously cultural front, Aunt Fanny was a great subscriber to the Victorian fashion for lecture evenings known as 'Lion Parties'. By the time they came to live in Blackheath, Clare and Eileen were considered old enough to attend these, and they sat entranced while one intrepid lady traveller, dressed in a long black dress and bonnet, gave an account of her thrilling exploits in darkest Asia to a large crowd on the lawn. They also attended recitals in the concert hall of the Blackheath Conservatoire, where Eileen was continuing her violin studies under the expert guidance of the violinist and conductor Alfred Burnett; she was eventually invited to join the staff as a part-time violin tutor.

There was no lack of romantic interest at Brooklands, as a girl never quite knew whom she might meet next. At one of Aunt Fanny's many At Homes Clare met and fell in love with one of her Peek cousins, Francis Daukes, but he did not love her and went off to marry someone else and eventually become the Bishop of Plymouth. Another source of friends was the seemingly endless stream of young men and women that would turn up at Brooklands with their hockey sticks over their handlebars to challenge the Kidd Team to a hockey match on one of their meadows. There was no qualification as to age or gender, and ignorance of the rules was certainly no disqualification, despite the fact that one of the regular players was Harry Tennant who, as well as being an incorrigible playboy, was also a hockey international.

* * *

In all of her many projects, Aunt Fanny knew that with Clare she could rely on a safe and sensible pair of hands. It was Clare who was there to help with the 'Toye children' who had walked up to Brooklands in crocodile-formation from their barrack-like orphanage – sad little figures in their coarse linen skirts and jackets and straw bonnets – and it was Clare who fished one of the little girls out of the pond and sent her home in the prettiest dress she had ever known while her own dried out. It was Clare who was there to welcome the twenty or so 'Old Women' brought by Miss Distant from the four small houses she ran in a run-down street in Deptford. Clare would wheel them around the garden in their bath chairs and listen to their stories, the Russian ex-governess practising her French on Clare, and the genteel manageress of a shop in Regent Street telling her how she had lost her position when she was no longer able to dye her hair.

Joseph too had noticed that Clare, who was by now twenty-two years old, seemed to be less frivolous and certainly less obsessed by the idea of finding a husband than most young women of her age. She was clearly possessed of a compassionate heart and a determination for social justice that mirrored his own, and he felt it was time to put these to more effective use. He discussed the matter with his son-in-law, and as a result Jack invited Clare to come and work as an assistant in his surgery. She accepted the offer with alacrity.

For a couple of years Clare worked hard in Uncle Jack's surgery in Shooters Hill Road. Although much of her work was secretarial and administrative, she would occasionally be required to accompany her uncle on home visits and was able to see for herself the glaring inequality in people's living conditions. She was making herself useful, not to say indispensable, to Uncle Jack but she was soon frustrated at not being able to do more to alleviate the misery she encountered, particularly among the women and children. Although Jack had got into the habit of handing over to Clare some of the more simple medical tasks, he knew, and she knew too, that there was a limit to what he could entrust to a woman with no formal training. The solution was simple; Clare would undergo the necessary training and qualify as a children's nurse.

With Clare's Aunt Mary having just qualified as a doctor, there was no objection in the family to the female members taking up a career, particularly if that career followed a serious medical discipline rather than some vaguely philanthropic or artistic pursuit, as was becoming more acceptable among the gentility. Some fifty years earlier Florence Nightingale had founded her training school for nurses with the money given to her by a grateful nation following the Crimean War. Before that the sick poor had been cared for in hospital by ignorant, sometimes degraded women. But with Florence Nightingale the era of modern nursing had dawned, and had already begun to be popular among women of higher social class. So long as it was unpaid, nursing was regarded as an acceptable activity for a young woman of breeding, particularly since the way it was set up in those days did not conflict with the correct social hierarchies. It was also one of the few ways that she could escape the monotonous round of domestic and social activities – and perhaps it was this that most appealed to Clare.

Sources

Lewisham Local Studies Library.

McCall, Dorothy. op. cit.

Rhind, Neil. *Blackheath Village & Environs*. Bookshop Blackheath Ltd, 1983.

Tarleton, Alfred. *About Deptford*. Nassau Press, 1897.

Chapter 5
Chosen Career

God how simple is the prescription for a happy life, to do what we
have to do out of love for the thing.

Karel Kapek

Clare's decision to specialise in children's nursing rather than general
nursing was very much in tune with the developing interest in babies and
infants that was current in Edwardian England, this interest ranging
from the scientific to the practical to the downright romantic. In his play
The Water Babies, written in 1904, Lewis Carroll was asking his audience
to believe that 'when the first baby laughed for the first time, the laugh broke
into a thousand pieces, and they all went skipping about, and that was the
beginning of fairies.' Indeed, so widespread was the growing sentimentality
about children that *The Illustrated London News* felt compelled to voice
its objection to this new 'cult of the child' in an article entitled 'His Majesty
the Baby'.

Meanwhile, in the scientific field, which of course was where Clare's
interest lay, great progress had been made in the field of paediatrics, which
had gained recognition as a specialised area of medicine in 1902. In her
Handbook of Nursing for the Home and the Hospital, which had for a long
time been regarded as the children's nurse's Bible, Catherine Wood, a
pioneer of children's nursing, had written:

> About forty years ago, little children were hardly thought of as
> needing special nursing or treatment; they were either forgotten or
> passed over in the mass of patients that crowded into the general
> hospitals. They died as little infants in thousands, trampled down
> under feet in the race for life, or they grew up stunted and deformed,
> dragging on a weary, sickly existence, uncheered by the laughter or
> gaiety of childhood, unsolaced by the tender love of mother. If they
> claimed their right to the great medical charities of our city, their

wee forms, strangely out of place in the large beds in the large wards, could hardly enforce attention; they were looked on as intruders and treated accordingly; the child laughter or the child cry jarred on the older patients; and the little sufferer learnt to bear its pain in silence, and was content to utter its plaint unheard. The doctors hardly knew how to handle these tiny frames. It was something like auscultating a turkey or percussing a goose; and their unspoken language of disease was hard to interpret.

Dr Charles West had taken up the challenge in 1852 by founding the Hospital for Sick Children in Great Ormond Street, and of him Catherine Wood, who herself became Lady Superintendent of that institution, eulogises (with contemporary sentimentality):

The little children are weaving a crown for him; and each little soul that wings its flight from those walls carries a leaf with it to place there, or each little pair of feet that patters out of its doors to tread again the road of life, walks in his strength who has pleaded and won its cause.

By 1909, when Clare was considering entering the profession, there were no fewer than eight children's hospitals in London[1], all based on the Great Ormond Street model and all following the two-year course designed by Catherine Wood for the training of children's nurses. The Hospital for Sick Children in Great Ormond Street had attracted support from the upper echelons of society from its earliest days; its reputation as a training establishment was high and its funding secure, and one would have thought it the obvious choice for Clare. But Joseph had a close friend, Dr Alexander Jex-Blake, who was Physician to Out-patients at The Victoria Hospital for Children, and so that is where it was decided Clare should enrol as a Private Probationer.

* * *

The Victoria Hospital for Children had been opened in Tite Street, Chelsea, in 1886 by the Prince and Princess of Wales, and at the time of Clare's arrival in 1909 its Patroness was Princess Louise, later to become

---

[1] Belgrave; East London; Evelina; Great Ormond Street; Paddington Green; Queen Alexandra's; Royal Waterloo; and Victoria.

the Duchess of Argyll. A year later this forceful lady succeeded in persuading her brother and his wife, recently crowned King George V and Queen Mary, to join her as Patrons of the hospital[1]. Princess Louise paid regular visits to the hospital and seems to have had a particular interest in its interior décor. When her offer of four large framed pictures of The Four Seasons to brighten up the entrance hall was turned down 'on sanitary grounds', the Princess came up with the idea of a *Water Babies* frieze to be painted directly onto the walls. This the Committee of Management found acceptable and recorded in its Minutes HRH's suggestion 'that the clouds in the *Water Babies* mural proposed for the entrance hall be increased from 3ft 6ins to 4ft 11ins to enable the decorative band to come in line with the door.'

In common with all hospitals at the time, the financial survival of the Victoria Hospital relied on a combination of private donations, fees received for the training of private nurse probationers and various types of voluntary activity. The 1909 Annual Report records a donation of £25 from Chelsea Football Club, along with numerous endowments, legacies and gifts from trusts. In 1910 a donation is recorded from Harrods, and the annual ball at the Princes Rooms made £133. In 1911 donations were substantially reduced or withdrawn entirely because of heavy taxation that year and the fear of further costs if the contributory scheme for sickness insurance made its way successfully through Parliament. As well as financial donations, both patients and staff enjoyed a variety of gifts and treats from time to time. There was a tea party and Punch & Judy show in the wards to celebrate King George V's coronation[2], and at Christmas the Queen presented each child with a box of chocolates, the King meanwhile providing the staff with game from the royal estates. There was a most active Ladies' Association, whose members not only engaged in fundraising, but were also to be seen visiting the wards each morning determined to 'educate and amuse' the unfortunate young patients. What the nurses, in their crisp sterile uniforms, made of so many furs, wraps and stoles swirling around their patients can only be imagined.

Details of the income and expenditure of the hospital are laid out most precisely in the minutes of the Committee of Management, who

---

[1] These royal connections, together with the smart Chelsea address, seem to have ensured that the hospital did not suffer the fate of many other children's hospitals over the next few years, lack of funding leading them to be absorbed by larger general hospitals. The Victoria did not finally close its doors until 1964.
[2] which was also celebrated by illuminating the entire hospital.

Balcony of the Victoria Hospital for Children, Chelsea

appear to have been incapable of delegating responsibility for even the smallest amounts of money. As a result, the minutes for the years that Clare spent at the Victoria are peppered with the name of a Mrs Day, who as Housekeeper was obliged to put in endless requests; for the pantry to be repainted at a cost of £7.10s; for a Pulvo vacuum cleaner at £16; and for the walls above the dado in the corridors to be finished in Ripolin at a cost of £4.15s. Her request for the cook's annual wages to be increased from £32 to £34 was deferred for a year and only granted then because Mrs Day agreed to replace the charwoman (wages £16 per annum) with a ward maid (£12 per annum). Similarly, it was the Committee of Management that had to agree the purchase of vital provisions for the hospital such as coal (18/9d per ton), flour (1/7 ¾d a stone) and bread (5d for a 4lb loaf).

The Victoria Hospital was an impressive redbrick building, each of its wards opening onto one of the extensive balconies that provided the 'open-air treatment' that was de rigueur at that time – the air being about as polluted and smog-ridden as it could possibly be. The stated aim of the hospital was 'the care of poor children from infancy to twelve years old in the case of boys, and fourteen in the case of girls.' The 104 beds and cots, divided into six large and airy wards, were each funded by a private endowment sufficient to cover the in-patient cost of £1.6s 1½d per week, the name of the benefactor appearing on a plaque at the head of each bed. Each ward was heated by two coal fires, which the ordinary Nurse Probationers had to ensure were kept burning night and day, and a trolley was provided for the ward maid to remove the ashes each morning. When Clare arrived, iron ladders had just been erected on the outside of the building so that the chimneys could be swept from the top, avoiding the need for sweeps to tramp around among the patients twice a year.

Upon admission, patients were required to bring with them a comb, brush, towel and soap, and for 3d per week the hospital would provide clean linen. Visiting hours were from 3 o'clock to 4 o'clock on Sundays only, and a notice was posted informing relations that visiting tickets would be withdrawn if they attempted to break the rule forbidding presents of food or fruit or if they tried to jump the queue by climbing over the turnstiles at the exit door. One of the more compassionate young doctors suggested in 1910 that parents be admitted into the first recovery room to attend their children after operations, but this was not considered desirable by the Committee of Management.

* * *

This was the hospital where, on 3rd April 1909, Clare Hedley-Peek was enrolled as a Private Probationer (previously known as a Lady-Pupil) for a fee of 52 guineas per annum payable quarterly in advance. The fee covered board and lodging but not laundry, and she was required to provide her own uniform, which nevertheless had to be of 'a pattern sanctioned for use in the Hospital.' The Hospital Rules stated that a Private Probationer, who should be no less than 21 years old and no more than 35, 'must provide evidence as to character, state of health and general fitness, disposition and temperament for performing the duties of a Nurse.' During the period of training, courses of lectures would be given by the Medical Officers in elementary anatomy, physiology and medical and surgical nursing, and instruction would be given by the Matron, Housekeeper and ward sisters in the management and nursing of sick children and in the cooking and preparation of their food. Examinations would be held from time to time, at which attendance was obligatory. Once she had completed her training, a Private Probationer would automatically become a Sister and might even go on to become a matron one day if she so wished.

The majority of trainees, however, were known simply as Nurse Probationers. These women came largely from a working-class background and saw nursing as a passport to economic independence and freedom. Since hospitals were run very much like convents, the women would also gain a level of social respectability, and their uniform would ensure that this was so[1]. Nurse probationers were provided with their uniform, accommodation and laundry (as well as tea and sugar) and were also paid a small wage. Although they could have earned more in a factory, these women knew that nursing could be a much longer-term career, offering greater mobility and a range of positions in hospitals, schools or private homes. These Probationers would not normally become Sisters at the end of their period of training.

The nurses' motto at the Victoria Hospital was '*in arduis fidelis*', and it would seem from the Nurses' Register that the Probationers' regime was so arduous that many of them were not able to remain faithful to the task for the full two years. In the same week that Clare enrolled, three other probationers also started the training course; Gladys Teague and Bessie Keable survived only two months, and Margaret Wood left after one year. In fact, the majority of those who embarked on the training did not stay the course, the reasons given in the Register for their premature departure ranging from 'Did not like the work' to 'Had flat feet', and from 'Left to be an organist' to 'Stole a pillow.' Many probationers left to be married, the married state not being regarded as compatible with the duties or ethos of a hospital ward.

* * *

Although Clare was no stranger to hard work, she must have found the days long, tiring and highly regimented. When on day duty, she had to leave the nurses' home in time for arrival on the ward by 7.35 am. Each Probationer was responsible for seven or eight children, and although these had been given breakfast and their beds made by the out-going night staff, they still had to be washed, changed, hair combed (in 80% carbolic), and their temperature taken. Once the patients were in good order, the area around their beds had to be swept, the brass cot knobs polished and the locker tops scrubbed. All of this had to be completed by 10 am, when the nurses would stand by their beds and the ward would lapse into deep silence as the Resident Medical Officer and House Surgeon

---

[1] When working in Brixton some years later, Clare was approached one night by a rather threatening-looking man. When he saw her uniform he muttered 'Sorry, nurse,' and moved on.

Ward in the Victoria Hospital for Children, Chelsea

would sweep into the ward to do their rounds. Throughout the day, medicines and stimulants had to be administered at the prescribed hours, poultices and fomentations changed and temperatures taken. Dinner had to be laid on each child's 'board' by 12 pm and then cleared away, after which toys would be given out at 2 pm and removed in time for tea to arrive at 4 pm. Operations generally took place in the afternoon, and Probationers were expected to assist at operations carried out on any patients in their care. Fainting on such occasions was taken extremely seriously and could result in a delay in qualifying. At 5 pm beds had to be made up for the night, draw-sheets taken out and shaken, and night-gowns and jackets changed. Probationers on day duty were free to leave the ward at around 6 pm.

Night duty began at 8 pm, when Probationers had to ensure all ward windows and ventilators 'street side' were closed, trolleys prepared, fires made up, hearths cleaned and breakfast trays made ready. At 11.30 pm one of them relieved the Staff Nurse on duty on her floor and at 12.30 am brought the night Sister her supper tray. After a half-hour break for their own supper (consisting mainly of sardines or an egg they had to boil themselves), they helped with feeds in the busier wards, brought Sister her cup of coffee at 3.30 am, and then began to prepare the bread and dripping for the patients' breakfast, dust out the bread pail and tidy the kitchen. Any spare time was to be spent mending the patients' little red and blue flannel vests and jackets, and 'definitely not reading novels in the kitchen.' A Probationer on night duty could leave the ward at 7 am and was to be in bed in the nurses' home by 12 pm.

The nurses' home itself afforded virtually no respite from the almost military regime that reigned on the ward, and even for the Private Probationers, who enjoyed slightly greater comfort and freedom, every aspect of life there was subject to some rule or regulation. Beds had to be stripped and windows opened before breakfast; nurses were not allowed to visit each other's rooms; there was to be no food in the bedrooms, no extra furniture, pictures or 'adornments' brought in and certainly no spirit lamps. Nurses were not allowed to turn on the bath tap and then leave the bathroom, they were not to loiter or talk loudly on the staircase or in the passages. And so it went on. As far as time-off was concerned, Probationers in general were allowed to go out for two hours a day (the time varying each day) and were lucky if they were given one weekend a month in which to return home. In this regard, the fee-paying Private Probationers probably fared slightly better.

* * *

As far as the patients were concerned, it is clear that children's hospitals in those days existed to provide care for sick rather than sickly children. The conditions listed in the Annual Reports when Clare was training are all acute cases such as bronchial pneumonia, lung tuberculosis, meningitis, inguinal hernias and middle-ear infections. The most common operations were tonsillectomies and what were delicately referred to by the nurses as 'circums'. Because of their somewhat precarious financial situation and the fact that funding was directly related to the number of patients treated, it was crucial for a hospital to be able to report a high patient turnover, and in the year Clare began her training, the Victoria recorded an astonishing total of 19 038 outpatients and 1270 admissions. So that beds could be vacated as swiftly as possible, most children's hospitals had an attached convalescent home, usually in the country and often by the sea, despite the fact that these only added to the financial strain. The Victoria had two such homes in Kent – one at Broadstairs and one at Biggin Hill. Another reason for removing patients to a convalescent home was that there seemed little point in returning them to the domestic circumstances which had often made them ill in the first place. The Annual Report for

1909 also admits unashamedly that:

> … some chronic cases of consumption and many cases of rickets and hip-joint disease and of scrofulous disease of the spine and of the joints are refused, either because they are incurable or because they only need rest for many months or years and seaside air.

In addition to long hours on the ward, probationers were required to do a certain amount of study in their free time and attend all lectures given by the various Medical Officers. These lectures, in subjects such as anatomy and physiology, were held somewhat unfortunately at 8.30 in the evening when everyone was fairly exhausted. From time to time viva examinations would be held by the Medical Officers with Matron presiding and ringing a little bell every seven minutes to indicate to the Probationers that it was time to move on to the next one.

* * *

This then was Clare's world for the next two years – a world far removed from the leisure and freedom of the days in Outwood and Blackheath. When she could snatch a couple of free hours, she might accompany one of the other Probationers on an outing to the park or a walk along the Embankment (dressed in the regulation long cloak and bonnet with large bow under the chin), and on half-days off there might be a visit to the theatre or a concert in the nearby Albert Hall. A strong camaraderie developed among the women with whom she now shared her life; everyone covered for everyone else's mistakes and some long-lasting friendships were forged.

Sources

Chelsea Local Studies Library.

Great Ormond Street Hospital Archives, London.

London Metropolitan Archives.

St George's Tooting Archives, London.

BURDETT, Sir Henry. *Burdett's Hospitals and Charities.* 1928.

LOMAX, Elizabeth. *Small and Special: The Development of Hospitals for Children in Victorian Britain.* 1996.

WOOD, Catherine J. *A Handbook of Nursing for the Home and the Hospital.* Cassell, Petter & Galpin, 1878.

Ibid. *The Training of Nurses for Sick Children – Nursing Record*, 6th December 1888.

Chapter 6
The Two Midwives

England will never again be a happy and secure nation until every child is born fortunate because born in England. The misery and hopelessness of one section of our people, the dissatisfaction of others, are a proof not that we are a poor nation but that we do not know how to use our riches ... I cannot respect any man who is content to enjoy a comfort and security that others of his countrymen have not.

Civil Journey, Storm Jameson

A few months after Clare began her training at the Victoria Hospital for Children, a new Probationer named Winifred Morris arrived. She was four years older than Clare and a full head shorter, and the two women became instant friends, calling each other by their surnames as was the practice among nurses in those days. Winifred decided to shorten Clare's name to 'Hedley' to make it more manageable, and from now on we shall refer to the couple as they did one another – Hedley and Morris.

Morris's father, Huson, was born in Kensington in 1848. He was a member of the London Stock Exchange and was a keen amateur cricketer (according to MCC records a middle-order right-hand batsman and right-hand fast medium round-arm bowler), playing in a first-class match for the MCC against Lancashire at Lord's in 1868. In 1876 Huson Morris married Elizabeth Webster and together they had six children, of whom Winifred, born in 1882, was the fourth. When the children were still quite young, Huson found himself in financial difficulties and decided to move the family from their home in Hayes, Kent, to St Jean de Luz in the south-west of France, where life was considerably cheaper[1]. Links with England were not severed, however; there were frequent visits home to the house in Hayes, and the two boys, Arthur and Norman, were educated at Charterhouse school in Surrey.

---

[1] And where he was to die in 1924.

Of the six Morris children, the eldest, Ella, had been married in 1900 to Walter Preston from the village of Highgrove near Tetbury; he owned a thriving transport manufacturing company[1]. Norman, the youngest, married Una O'Dwyer, daughter of Michael O'Dwyer who was to be responsible for the Amritsar massacre of 1919 (he was murdered at Caxton Street by Udham Singh in 1940). The second son, Arthur, died tragically at the age of twenty-one in Paris; his father was so grief-stricken that he was taken along on Ella and Walter's honeymoon. Hilda, Winifred and Edith remained spinsters, and it is possible that Winifred's decision to join the nursing profession at the comparatively late age of twenty-eight was based on the view that her marital prospects were by now growing slim. Such a belief would have been reinforced by her father, who had told her from an early age that she reminded him of 'a sack of potatoes.'

* * *

Hedley completed the two years' training as a children's nurse in April 1911, Morris the following September, but the two women were not to receive their certificates for another eight years. The first attempt to create a scheme for the registration of nurses had been launched in 1893 by the newly-formed Royal British Nurses' Association but had unaccountably met with opposition from nurse training schools in London, many provincial hospital authorities and even Florence Nightingale who held that:

> … as personal qualities are of first importance in a Nurse and cannot be registered, it would be misleading to allow Nurses or the public to imagine that any scheme of State Registration would indicate the fitness of any woman registered to act as a desirable attendant on the sick[2].

However, Ethel Bedford Fenwick, a one-time matron of St Bartholomew's Hospital, continued to fight for registration for most of the first two decades of the 20th century. The Nurses' Registration Act was finally passed in 1919, its passage through Parliament given a strong following wind by public recognition of the contribution of nurses to the war effort, both at home and abroad. The inclusion of children's nurses on the register had been hugely contentious, with many people, including Mrs Bedford

---

[1] J. Stone & Co. It later merged with Platt & Co. to create Stoneplatt.
[2] Memorandum on the State Registration of Nurses issued by the CHCL in 1904.

Fenwick, not considering them fully trained nurses at all. After several proposed amendments to the Bill, children's nurses were given their own supplementary Children's Register, to which Hedley's and Morris's names were added.

As their training at the Victoria Hospital had progressed, it had become increasingly apparent to Hedley and Morris that many of the cases they were encountering were the direct result of the poor care and nutrition the child had received in his early years or in some cases from mistakes made in the management of his birth. It seemed logical to them, therefore, that to complete their training, they should also qualify as midwives, and so in the Autumn of 1911 the two women enrolled at the Training School for Midwives and Monthly Nurses of the General Lying-In Hospital in York Road, Lambeth.

* * *

The practice and profession of midwifery has always been one of the battle-grounds of medicine and is still much fought over today. The word 'midwife' comes from the old English 'mid wyf', meaning 'with a woman', and since the beginning of time women have been assisted in their confinement by other wise women[1]. Unfortunately, by the mid-nineteenth century, the midwife in England had taken on the garrulous, gin-tippling and distinctly unprofessional image of Mrs Sairey Gamp in Charles Dickens' *Martin Chuzzlewit* and was seen as an undesirable working class woman, out for personal gain at the expense of her patients. Among the uneducated, child-birth was surrounded by bizarre superstitions; mirrors were covered so that the child would not be born blind, and to hasten the delivery all knots would be untied and drawers opened.

As a result of this, the medical profession, which was highly organised and exclusively male, was attempting to take over midwifery and render obsolete the traditional female midwife. In her '*Introductory notes on lying-in institutions*' of 1871, Florence Nightingale had made a passionate bid to halt this medical take-over of childbirth:

Here is a matter so pressing, so universally recognised, viz. the preferable attendance of women upon women in midwifery, that it may really be summed up thus: although every woman would prefer

---

[1] The French for midwife is 'sage femme'. The Germans have the somewhat more graphic title 'die Hebamme', meaning the woman who heaves!

a woman to attend upon her in her lying-in, and in diseases peculiar to her and her children, yet the woman does not exist, or hardly exists to do it. Midwives are so ignorant that it is almost a term of contempt.… The rich woman cannot find fully qualified women, but only men, to attend her, and the poor woman only takes unqualified women because she cannot afford to pay well-qualified men.

Nightingale goes on to compare the mortality rates among women delivered in the male-dominated lying-in hospitals and those delivered at home: 34 deaths per 1000 in hospital and 4.7 per 1000 at home. According to her, the dramatically higher death rate in hospitals was due to the increased risk of puerperal disease when lying-in women, who were anyhow more susceptible to infection, were crowded at various stages of their confinement into the same room – a room which had often been used for too long without cleansing and thorough airing. The other causes she cites are the proximity of midwifery wards to post mortem theatres, the admittance of medical students from general hospitals and anatomy schools, and the practice of allowing the same attendants to act in infirmary wards and lying-in wards. Midwifery wards in general hospitals should, in Nightingale's opinion, be closed down immediately.

Having become the figurehead of the new standard of female nurse, Florence Nightingale then campaigned for the creation of a new breed of fully qualified 'nurse midwife' who could fend off the potentially lethal attentions of the doctors. The mother would be delivered either in her own home, or else in a small lying-in institution that replicated home conditions but with scrupulous attention to ventilation and cleanliness. Although nursing had become an accepted profession for a woman of breeding, midwifery on the other hand had only recently been regarded as a suitable career for a lady. When Dame Rosalind Paget, one of 'Miss Nightingale's Young Ladies', decided to specialise in the field, one of her friends, more than a little embarrassed by her activities, was heard to say, 'My dear, I wish there were another word for you, it would be so awkward if we used it just when the footman came in to put on coals.'

* * *

The General Lying-In Hospital, where Hedley and Morris trained, was founded in 1765 by a Dr John Leake to 'provide relief for poor women, particularly the wives of soldiers and sailors.' In 1830 it had been incorporated by Royal Charter and moved into rather imposing premises in York Road, Lambeth. The main purpose of the Lying-in Hospital was to provide midwives to deliver patients in their own homes, but 'respectable married women, whose circumstances compel them to ask for aid in the form of charity' were also received as in-patients during their confinement. This meant that a school for midwives and monthly nurses could be established,

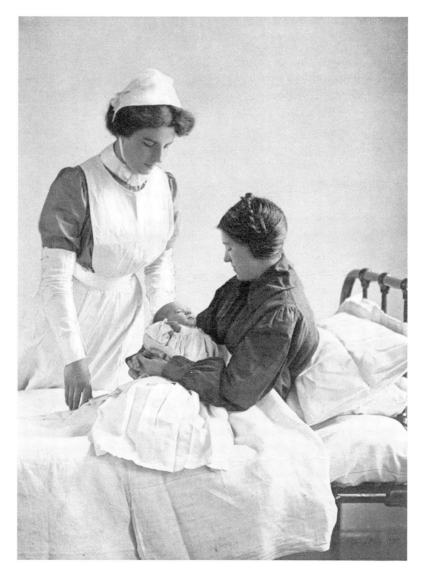

Hedley with newly delivered mother, General Lying-In Hospital, Lambeth

where the trainees could observe and practise the skills of midwifery in the most up-to-date hospital conditions. The 1911 annual report notes that 'in exceptional cases, *unmarried* women who are found by the Committee of Management, upon careful investigation, to have shown general good conduct and to be objects of real commiseration, are not refused the benefits of the Hospital,' but this magnanimous gesture on the part of the Committee only applied to the first such confinement.

The General Lying-In Hospital was proud of its reputation of being the most modern maternity hospital in the country, as it had been the first to practise the aseptic method of midwifery promoted by Ignaz Semmelweiss. Semmelweiss was a Hungarian Jewish physician at a maternity hospital in Vienna, which had two separate sections, one staffed by doctors and nurses and the other by midwives and nurses. He was puzzled by the fact that the mortality rate among mothers in the section staffed by doctors was 18%, whilst that in the midwives' section was less than 1%. On investigation, Semmelweiss found that doctors were going from the post mortem room, where they dissected women who had died from puerperal fever, straight to the delivery rooms, where they then delivered new babies and often gave the infection to their mothers. By persuading the doctors to wash their hands in chlorinated lime water after they had been in the post mortem room, the death rate in the doctors' section soon fell to 1%. This expedient was warmly welcomed by the younger doctors but hugely resented by the older ones, who got Semmelweiss sacked from his job. He died shortly afterwards in 1865 in a mental hospital.

In common with all hospitals at that time, the General Lying-In was largely dependent on charitable donations, and in the year that Hedley and Morris started their training, the annual report records a gift of 3 guineas from Mrs Joseph Kidd. Further gifts that year, from more illustrious donors, include game from HM Queen Alexandra, garments from HRH the Princess Royal and two armchairs from Lady Blandford. The Duchess of Buccleuch gave twenty-one coronation seats for nurses, to which the American millionaire William Waldor Astor added a further ten. Other donations include books and periodicals, fish, six copies a day of the *Daily Telegraph*, eggs, elastic stockings, coronation mugs and egg cups, and tickets for the Rose Show.

In the case of trained nurses such as Hedley and Morris, the midwifery course at the Lying-In Hospital was completed in just 4 months, during which time they lived in the hospital. The total fee for the course was 28 guineas. Along with the other trained nurses, Hedley and Morris served in rotation in the mothers' wards, the nurseries, the labour wards, the ante-natal clinics and on the district. Under the rules laid down by the Central Midwives Board, they had to deliver personally, under supervision, a minimum of twenty normal cases of childbirth during the 4 month period, and they would be summoned in rotation until this number of deliveries was achieved. Whenever possible they would observe all deliveries, including the abnormal cases that were delivered by the physician accoucheur himself or, in the case of Caesareans, by a surgeon who had been called in from nearby St Thomas's Hospital. Medical lectures were given by one of the attending physicians, and classes in midwifery by one of the Sisters or by Matron herself – the somewhat terrifying Miss Watkins.

Each day, when one of the attending physicians started on his rounds, a bell would be rung and all the pupil-midwives would leave their work – if they were able – and follow behind the physician, listening to his comments on each of the patients. A bell was also rung whenever a woman was about to be delivered in one of the labour rooms, and all the available pupil-midwives would file into the labour room, where the Sister in charge would select one of them to conduct the delivery under supervision. Once assigned a maternity case of her own, the pupil-midwife would follow straight through until the mother was back in her own bed, as it was regarded as essential to give the mother consecutive care by one person and never to leave her alone. This meant that Hedley and Morris were often on duty for long hours at a stretch, but if the mother did not deliver until after midnight, they were allowed to sleep until noon the next day. There were no holidays and no half-days off.

In February 1912 Hedley and Morris succeeded in passing the examination set by the Central Midwives Board and were awarded the certificate that entitled them to practise as midwives 'under the rules and regulations laid down in pursuance of the Midwives Act 1902.' Their names were added to the 'Approved Midwives List' of the General Lying-In Hospital, and from now on they were sent out each day to work in the district, Hedley often finding herself in the familiar territory of Bermondsey and Deptford. After a year she was promoted to the post of Ward and Night Sister in the hospital, while Morris continued her district work.

True to its founder's original vision, the Lying-In Hospital concentrated most of its efforts on providing relief to women living in the poorer parts of the city, particularly in the south-east of London. A description of some of the more appalling housing conditions in the Borough of Deptford has already been given, and now we must return there to take a closer

No. *35457* Date *Feb. 19th 1912*

Central Midwives Board.

(2 Edw. VII. ch. 17.)

We hereby Certify

That *Clare Sybil Peck*

having passed the Examination of the Central Midwives Board,
and having otherwise complied with the rules and regulations
laid down in pursuance of the Midwives Act, 1902, is entitled
by law to practise as a Midwife in accordance with the provisions of the said Act and subject to the said rules and
regulations.

E Parker Young } Members
R Paget } of the
  } Board.

G W Duncan Secretary.

look at what life was like for the women and children who lived in its fifty-three miles of dingy streets. According to R. S. Rowntree's 'minimum needs scale' calculated in 1901, more than four-fifths of the families in Deptford's East Ward were living in a state of 'primary poverty', that is to say that their total earnings were insufficient to obtain the minimum necessities for 'the maintenance of mere physical efficiency'. To understand this term it would be well to quote Rowntree's explanation in full:

> The members of such families must never spend a penny on railway fare or omnibus. They must never go into the country unless they walk. They must never purchase a halfpenny newspaper or spend a penny to buy a ticket for a popular concert. They must write no letters to absent children, for they cannot afford to pay the postage. They must never contribute anything to their church or chapel, or give anything to a neighbour which costs them money. The children must have no pocket money for dolls, marbles or sweets. The father must smoke no tobacco and must drink no beer. The mother must never buy any pretty clothes for herself or for her children, the character of the family wardrobe as for the family diet being governed by the regulation 'Nothing must be bought but that which is absolutely necessary for the maintenance of physical health, and what is bought must be of the plainest and most economical description'. Should a child fall ill, it must be attended by the parish doctor; should it die, it must be buried by the parish. Finally, the wage-earner must never be absent from his work for a single day. If any of these conditions are broken, the extra expenditure involved is met, and can only be met, by limiting the diet; or, in other words, by sacrificing physical efficiency.

Where there were no more than two children in the family, provided the wage-earner stayed in regular employment and earned the average wage of twenty shillings a week, it might have been just possible to live above the poverty line, but the majority of parents seemed completely incapable of limiting the size of their family or at least relating it to income. Although most of the women knew of some primitive (and usually unsuccessful) means of birth control, few of them were willing to practise this for fear that their men would only take greater advantage of them if they knew that sexual intercourse would not necessarily lead to the birth of more children. Added to the combination of small wages and large families was the problem of alcohol, which often soaked up the money that was needed for food and clothing. 'The characteristics of Monday morning in Deptford are bundles and jugs', wrote a social worker at the time. 'The former go to the pawnshop and the latter to the beer shop.' Gambling was another drain on the family finances, and it was not uncommon for a bookmaker to take £70 in less than two hours.

Most of the children in Deptford would have gone to school without breakfast if it had not been for local philanthropists, who handed out tickets to many of them entitling them to a mug of tea, a roll and a piece of cheese. Compulsory schooling meant that mothers had to provide their children with shoes so that they could go out in all weathers, but these often had holes right through them, so that children's feet were constantly wet and chilblained. The clothes they wore to school were little more than rags. The social reformer Margaret McMillan's pamphlet *Citizens of Tomorrow*, written about this time, records how doctors, having examined the children in one Deptford school, found 87% of them to be in an unsatisactory state, 34% being 'dirty in body and clothes' and 11% actually 'dirty and verminous'.

Hedley and Morris had been taught that the causes of infant mortality were, in order of importance, poverty, malnutrition, overcrowding, lack of sleep, poor hygiene, maternal inadequacy and lack of clothing. As they set out as nurse midwives to work on the district, they were only too well aware that there was a limit to what their expert ministrations could achieve. Many of the mothers they cared for were supplementing the family income with factory work or sweated labour, and Hedley and Morris knew that babies born to working mothers tended to weigh less than those who were at home and rested during pregnancy. They knew too that breast-fed babies usually survived better than those who were bottle-fed, and many of the mothers, having returned far too early to physically demanding work, soon lost the ability to breast-feed effectively. Add to that the appalling state of hygiene of many of the homes where these babies were delivered, and it was not difficult to understand why the infant mortality rate was so scandalously high. It was often with a heavy heart that the two midwives handed the weary mother another hungry mouth to feed, maybe with Margaret McMillan's words ringing in their ears: 'Who can tell what great men have died in their cradles?'.

For two years Hedley and Morris threw themselves tirelessly into their work, exchanging notes at the end of each day – or each night if there was a night-time delivery. The emotional support the couple could give one another was particularly important when there had been a still-birth which, even in the case of in-patient confinements, was not uncommon. The 1911 Annual Report of the hospital records 830 children born in the hospital, of which 35 were still-born and 17 died soon after birth. The figures for home-births assisted by Lying-In Hospital midwives were naturally higher than that, since no physicians or surgeons were at hand to take over in an emergency.

* * *

If it had been proved that infant mortality, which had by then been recognised as a national problem, was largely due to poor social conditions, surely something could be done, thought the two women – and the Women's Labour League thought likewise. The Women's Labour League had come into being in 1906 at a conference in Leicester, and was inaugurated the same year in London at a public meeting attended by Keir Hardie, who remained a staunch friend of the League. Unlike the Women's Social and Political Union, which was a militant suffrage movement (of which Mrs Pankhurst was a member), the League was created to represent the whole range of women's interests and responsibilities, and foremost among these were infant mortality and childcare. In 1908 the League had become affiliated to the Labour Party, and another warm supporter was Ramsay MacDonald, whose wife Margaret was one of the League's early leaders. Margaret felt strongly that the issues of home and children should be discussed politically and addressed by the Labour Party.

The League continually stressed the need for issues to be presented by women who had personal experience of them, rather than by politicians, insisting that 'it is most difficult to get reliable evidence ... theorising leads one astray'. And so in 1912 Hedley and Morris joined the by then 5000 League members, contributing useful first-hand experience to the discussions at their local branch meetings and providing material for leaflets to be handed out to working mothers which promoted measures of child welfare in the community. By the time Hedley and Morris joined the League, infant mortality had become one of the dominant issues, particularly after the death of Margaret MacDonald's baby son, David. Soon after the tragedy Margaret wrote:

These statistics of mortality among children have become unbearable to me. I used to be able to read them in a dull scientific way, but now I seem to know the pain behind each one. It is not true that other children can make it up to you, or that time heals the pain. It doesn't, it just grows worse and worse. We women must work for a world where little children will not needlessly die.[1]

When Margaret died just one year after her son, it seemed natural for the League to spend the funds raised in her memory on an experimental baby clinic – the first of its kind to be run and fully controlled by a national body of women. The clinic was open daily and did not require mothers to bring a letter of recommendation. Infants who were well were welcomed for preventive health advice, and those who were sick were treated free of charge. With the experience they had gained from both the Victoria Children's Hospital and the Lying-In Hospital, Hedley and Morris were able to give invaluable help and advice.

* * *

In the Spring of 1914, after two years' experience of delivering babies both in hospital and on the district, Hedley felt that she was ready to run her own lying-in institution and took over from a Miss Nieson as Principal of the Loughborough Park Midwifery and Nursing Institution in Brixton, South London, Morris joining her as Deputy Principal. In line with Florence Nightingale's recommendations, the Loughborough Park Institution was small and aimed to replicate the best of home conditions. There were only four beds to each ward and plenty of ventilation to protect the mothers from what were considered the 'excessively poisonous emanations from lying-in women brought together in institutions'. Floors and furniture were polished constantly, and there was frequent lime-washing of walls and ceilings to prevent infection. The delivery ward was in a quite separate part of the building.

Before closing this chapter, the modern reader might be intrigued to discover that in 1914 the lying-in period in a lying-in home lasted two weeks with the 'patient' remaining in bed until the twelfth day on a diet of easily digested foods such as beef tea, albumen water, white of egg, gruel, cocoa and weak tea. Once solids were introduced, these would consist of thin bread and butter or dry toast and a soft-boiled egg. The only visitor permitted in the first week was the husband, with other relatives being allowed in one at a time in the second week. *Sic tempora sic mores!*

---

[1] Labour Party Headquarters Archives – Subject Files.

Sources

Labour Party Headquarters Archives.

Royal College of Nursing Archives.

Women's Library, London.

BASHFORD, Alison. *Purity and Pollution: Gender, Embodiment and Victorian Medicine.* St Martin's Press Inc., New York, 1998.

BRADBURY, Elizabeth. *Margaret McDonald: Framework & Expansion of Nursery Education.* 1976.

COLLETTE, Christine. *For Labour and for Women.* Manchester University Press, 1989.

NIGHTINGALE, Florence. *Introductory Notes on Lying-in Institutions,* 1871.

TARLETON, Alfred. op. cit.

TOWLER, Jean & BRAMWELL, Joan. *Midwives in History and Society,* 1986.

Chapter 7
Nurses at War

Always remember that one is given by fate only one lifetime in which to work and live for humanity. There is no greater crime in my opinion than to renounce the world, no matter for what excuse.

Clive Branson, Bristish soldier in India

Hedley had been Principal of the Loughborough Park Midwifery and Nursing Institution for only a few months when, in August 1914, the First World War broke out. The effect of the separation of parents on babies and young children was now of great concern, as was the fact that some soldiers had not had the time, or possibly the inclination, to marry before departing for the Front. Since the law had no regard for children born out of wedlock, the upkeep of such children was fraught with difficulty. The League now turned its attention to this seemingly intractable problem, campaigning so that children born to parents who married after their birth would be declared legitimate, and that a woman should be able to get an affiliation order before the birth of her child. Although conscription was not to be introduced until 1916, a million volunteers had come forward by the end of the year for Kitchener's 'New Army', and Hedley and Morris found themselves frequently delivering babies whose fathers were either away fighting at the Front or had been killed.

Hedley and Morris continued to be passionate about their work as nurse midwives in one of the most deprived areas of London, but when it became clear that the war was not going to be 'over by Christmas' as people had originally hoped, they realised that there was now another more urgent call on their nursing skills. The Germans had completed their occupation of Belgium with astonishing speed, and the area of hostilities was growing larger by the week. Terrible stories were reaching England about the fate of civilians in the Flemish and French villages that the German army were deliberately devastating as they retreated before the early Allied counter-attacks, and there appeared to be a desperate shortage of nurses to care for these wretched individuals.

Whereas nursing had been established in England for some time as a serious and noble lay profession, in France it had until relatively recently been entirely in the hands of religious orders. In 1904 the Prime Minister, Émile Combes, had introduced legislation which would result in the complete separation of Church and State and which forbade 'the teaching of any kind by any Religious Order'. As a consequence, some 20 000 priests and nuns were unemployed – officially denied the right to teach – and although nuns continued to be allowed to practise as nurses, much Church property was confiscated, and vast numbers of religious communities were forced to leave the country. When the nuns left France they left behind a gap which could not instantly be filled, and by the time war broke out nursing had only just started to be taken up seriously as a lay profession. Clear about where their duty lay, Hedley and Morris wrote off to the appropriate authority to offer their services.

The Joint War Committee of the Red Cross (JWC) had been created in October 1914 to bring together the St John Ambulance Association and the British Red Cross Society, taking on responsibility for the Trained Nurses Department of both bodies. The JWC now received all requests for trained nurses to serve in both Home and Foreign Services and made arrangements for the nurses to be sent to wherever they were needed. After acquiring and returning all the necessary forms, Hedley and Morris were requested to appear before the Selection Board at 83 Pall Mall, the headquarters of the Joint Committee, where they were interviewed by Dame Sarah Swift, late Matron of Guy's Hospital and now Matron-in-Chief of the Joint Committee. After references had been taken up from the Matron of the Victoria Children's Hospital where they had trained, the two women's names were added to the Index of Trained Nurses of the JWC.

In the great surge of patriotism that was sweeping across the nation, large numbers of young women, particularly those from genteel and even aristocratic families, were offering their services abroad. Those with no nursing training signed up as members of the Voluntary Aid Detachment, known as VADs, and it was sometimes difficult to explain to these women, as well as to many of the trained nurses, that the Front was wherever there were sick and wounded. Wounded men were generally sent on their way to home hospitals within a few hours of being picked up on the battlefield, so that the women who were serving in the hospitals of Southampton or London were effectively working at the Front quite as much as their sisters in Flanders. If a nurse was particularly anxious to be sent abroad, however, she had to undergo a second interview with the Matron of the Foreign Service Department and, if successful, her name would be added to the List for Foreign Service. To be considered, she would need to have a good health certificate, a 'good personality' and a fair knowledge of languages, customs and life abroad. For Morris, who had spent most of her childhood in France, none of this presented a problem; Hedley, with only schoolgirl French, had rather greater difficulty. However, both of them passed the second interview successfully, were inoculated against typhoid and sent home to await instructions. Before being posted to France, Hedley had the great joy of delivering her sister, Eileen, of her first child, a son named Hedley Wilton[1].

In the middle of November 1915 Hedley and Morris's posting arrived; Hedley was to make herself ready to leave England on 11th December, and Morris would follow on ten days later. Their destination was the Western Front, but they were not to be told the precise location until after their arrival at the French Headquarters of the Joint War Committee in Boulogne. They had put in a request to work together and had been told that this should not be difficult to arrange. There was a great deal to organise in the following four weeks, and a fair amount of bureaucracy to be satisfied. After much additional form-filling, they finally procured their Permit for Travelling, together with a slip authorising them to present themselves at various offices, where they would be given a certificate, brassard (armband) and particulars of travel.

Nurses were expected to supply their own indoor uniform, which they were told should consist of dark blue cotton dresses, white aprons and regulation nurses' collars and cuffs, worn with a dark blue belt and army cap 'with double fold turned outward'. The outdoor uniform was provided by the JWC and consisted of a navy blue coat, with red facings on the collar and cuffs, red shoulder straps and JWC buttons. Navy blue straw

---

[1] Shortly before the war broke out Eileen had married Arthur Wilton Atkinson, the eldest son of a Blackheath family that had distinguished itself in the eyes of the Kidds by being able to field almost an entire hockey team, so numerous were its offspring. The Atkinsons lived in a most elegant house overlooking the Heath, and Eileen had become particularly friendly with one of the daughters, Marjorie, to whom she gave violin lessons at the Conservatoire. Shortly afterwards Eileen met and married Marjorie's eldest brother, Arthur. Hedley was delighted with her first nephew, and an enduring bond was forged between the little boy and the woman whose hands were the first to hold him. Thirty-two years later this nephew, after surviving three years in the Burma jungle with the Chindits, was to christen his first child Clare. I was his second daughter.

hats were to be worn in the summer and black felt ones in the winter, and a JWC badge was also given to them to wear on their outdoor coats. All of this had to be handed in when the nurse's duties were terminated. Discipline in terms of dress was clearly considered most important, and the following regulations were to be strictly observed:

> Only small hat pins to be worn and brassard securely pinned inside coat-pocket so that it may be shown if asked for. No caps, aprons, golf jerseys, veils or coloured or thin silk stockings are to be worn in the street. Sisters are permitted only to go without their coats on very hot days if they have a walking dress of navy blue, worn with gloves. Navy blue, black or brown mackintoshes may be worn on very wet days. No mufti whatsoever may be worn on any occasion. A suitcase and hold-all only allowed for Foreign Service. No cameras allowed.

On 11th December Hedley made her way to Victoria Station, where she was given her tickets and passport only an hour before the train was due to depart. She and the nurses travelling with her were met at Folkestone by transport officials, who escorted them onto the troop ship, or more accurately the cross-channel ferry that was serving as a troop ship, for the short journey across the channel to France. Peering through the December sea mist for her first sight of France, Hedley would have been greeted by the seemingly endless white line of the cliff-top encampments, which stretched right down the coast from Calais to Deauville, marquee hospitals filled to capacity with wounded soldiers awaiting transportation back to England. After landing in Boulogne, the nurses were taken straight to the head-quarters of the Joint War Committee. There they were informed of their posting by the Principal Matron, Nora Fletcher, who was responsible for allocating the nursing staff to wherever reinforcements had been requested. Hedley was told that she would be serving on 'Madam O'Gorman's FAU Isle of Wight Barge, currently moored on the Canal de la Haute Colme near Bergues'. Morris would be joining her there ten days later.

* * *

The letters 'FAU' stood for the Friends' Ambulance Unit, an organisation set up at the beginning of the war by a group of Quakers. Though independent, the FAU worked as an integral part of the Joint War

Committee, whose Boulogne headquarters kept it constantly supplied with medical personnel. Quakers as a religious body have always held that war is wrong, and the use of force contrary to Christian principles. However, a large number of them were shocked by the monstrous explosion that had ripped Europe apart in August 1914 and resolved to participate in the struggle in some way that did not involve them becoming combatant. Having started off with a little company of forty-three men and eight small ambulances, by the end of the war they were running hospitals (in towns such as Dunkirk and Ypres), ambulance trains and hospital ships; they were also carrying out relief work in the destitute Flemish villages and conducting a preventive campaign against typhoid among the civilians there.

The 'Madam O'Gorman' referred to in Hedley's posting was a large, formidable Catholic woman in her mid-fifties from Shanklin on the Isle of Wight. Her full name was Flora O'Gorman, but for some reason she was known to all as Madam O'Gorman. Within one month of war being declared, Madam O'Gorman, who had extensive nursing experience, had enrolled with the British Red Cross and was sent to Antwerp. Here she had bought a large coal barge named the Secours Perpetuel, which she had converted into a hospital barge and re-christened 'The Isle of Wight'. On 10th October Antwerp surrendered to the Germans, and Madam O'Gorman was forced to abandon her barge and return to England or risk being interned[1].

Nothing daunted, Madam O'Gorman enrolled for a second time in December 1914 and this time was sent out to manage a team of eight British nurses and a number of VADs who were working at the Hôpital Elizabeth, a typhoid hospital set up by the Friends Ambulance Unit in Poperinghe, just over the Belgian border. Once the typhoid emergency had been contained, Madam O'Gorman decided that she could entrust her British nurses to Countess van den Steen, the Belgian woman who was responsible for the general management of the hospital, and made arrangements for her barge to be moved down the canal system from Antwerp to Dunkirk, where it could be used to care for the sick and wounded refugees that were flooding out of Belgium. The barge would be attached to another FAU hospital in Dunkirk, the Queen Alexandra, although Madam O'Gorman insisted that it remain a separate unit.

---

[1] She was later awarded the Mons Star, which was given to 'those who actually served under the fire of the enemy in France or Belgium between 5 August and 22 November 1914'.

Isle of Wight barge

By April 1915 the Western Front was moving closer to Dunkirk, and the Germans had started to shell the city. Not far away the second battle of Ypres was underway and Dunkirk was overwhelmed with wounded soldiers awaiting transport home to Britain. The Germans had started using chlorine gas for the first time, and the chlorine gas was not particular about whether it poisoned military or civilian lungs, so the FAU decided to set up another civilian hospital, this time at a safe distance from Dunkirk in the little town of Watten on the banks of the river Aa. Madam O'Gorman was to move her barge to this new location, where it would serve as a ward for male patients, and the female patients would be accommodated in four marquees erected in the meadows nearby. Six smaller tents were pitched alongside the marquees to provide accommodation for staff and stores.

By August Poperinghe too was coming under heavy shelling, and Countess van den Steen was obliged temporarily to evacuate the civilian patients from the Hôpital Elizabeth. It was decided to move the hospital sheds from Poperinghe to the Ferme de Rycke in Watten, not far from the barge and tent hospitals. By now the hospital in the meadow was looking for winter quarters, as the marquees were only really a practical solution

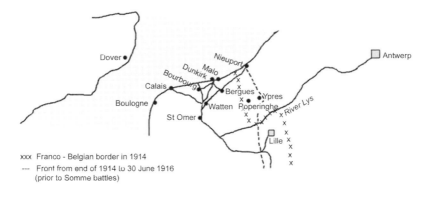

Map showing movement of barge, 1915–1918

during the summer months, and at the end of September it was decided to transfer all the women patients to the Hôpital Elizabeth annexe nearby. Male patients were to remain with Madam O'Gorman on the Isle of Wight barge. The two units were amalgamated to form one hospital for the care of Belgian and French sick and wounded, specialising in cases requiring particularly careful and lengthy treatment and receiving their patients from other hospitals in the area.

Before long doubts began to be expressed about whether the barge could provide suitable winter quarters, and within a couple of months a number of patients still under treatment were being discharged, some of them to return to the main hospital at Poperinghe. By the end of October there were only ten patients left on the barge, and that month only two operations had been performed. Madam O'Gorman decided that it was time to strike out alone and had the barge moved up the Canal de la Haute Colme to Petit Millebrugghe near Bergues. She had the barge registered as a separate field hospital with the Joint War Committee and immediately put in a request for two trained nurses.

Sources
British Red Cross Archives, London.

Imperial War Museum, London.

Isle of Wight Record Office, Newport, Isle of Wight.

Library of the Religious Society of Friends, London.

British Red Cross Society, Summaries of Work 1914 and 1915.

MEABURN, Tatham & JAMES, Miles (eds). *The Friends Ambulance Unit 1914–19*. The Swarthmore Press Ltd, 1920.

War Organisation of the British Red Cross Society & Order of St John of Jerusalem. *Official Reports of the Joint War Committee 1914–19*.

Chapter 8
The Hospital Barge

For God hath not given us the spirit of fear; but of power, and of love, and of a sound mind.

2 Timothy, 1:7

Within a few hours of arriving in Boulogne, Hedley was handed into a motor vehicle, already loaded up with medical and other supplies requested by Madam O'Gorman, and driven the fifty miles or so from Boulogne to the little village of Petit Millebrugghe, perched on the edge of the Canal de la Haute Colme near Bergues. There, lying peacefully moored to the canal bank under a row of bare-branched poplar trees, was a huge barge with the Red Cross emblem painted on its side.

Hedley had seen canal barges at home, but these had been no longer than 70 feet long; the Isle of Wight Barge was a massive 124 feet long by 16 feet wide. Originally open to the skies, a roof had been constructed the full length of the barge, with a raised canvas canopy at one end to shelter the gangway leading down to the accommodation below. Hedley had imagined that a barge interior would be dark and airless, and was much relieved to see that numerous windows had been set into the newly constructed roof to let in light and air. Together with its little chimney and its two flags, the French tricolor at one end and the Red Cross flag at the other, the Isle of Wight barge certainly looked like a serious ambulance unit.

If the exterior of the barge was impressive, the interior was even more so. After climbing down the gangway, Hedley found herself in a small anteroom, where she was greeted by Madam O'Gorman and the outgoing sister, Sister Robinson, and then through to what was surprisingly a sizeable and perfectly traditional hospital ward. The first thing that struck her was the cosy atmosphere in contrast to the December chill outside, the heat being provided by a Godin stove near the entrance to the ward. The walls, ceiling and beams had all been whitewashed, and a false floor had been constructed and covered with linoleum. Most of the windows in the roof had been thrown open to ensure sufficient ventilation for the patients, and the overall effect was one of space, light and airiness. Down each side of the ward there were thirteen iron hospital beds, each neatly covered with a floral counterpane, and on the wall above each bed hung the occupant's medical notes. A small cupboard next to each bed completed the furnishings, together with electric lights in pretty glass lampshades attached to the crossbeams.

The twenty-six beds were occupied by the oddest assortment of men and boys Hedley could possibly imagine, all of them Belgian refugees. The oldest must have been in his eighties and the youngest no more than eight years old, with a conspicuous lack of any men of combative age. Some of them were sitting on the edge of their bed with their own rather tattered jackets pulled over their hospital pyjamas, and these inspected her curiously, while others lay prostrate on their pillows and seemed quite oblivious of her arrival. Many of them had limbs in a splint, some had their head bandaged, several had large dressings strapped to their chest or abdomen.

If Hedley had assumed that this unexpectedly large ward occupied the full length of the barge, she was to be proved wrong. At the far end of the

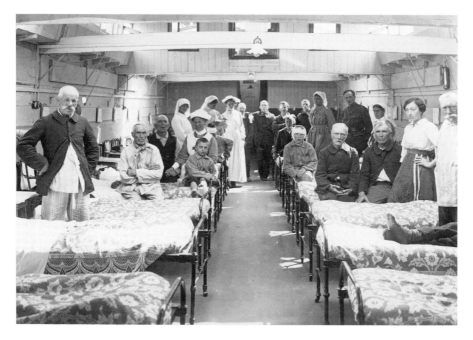

Isle of Wight barge interior

ward a door led into a narrow passage, again lit from above, with several doors leading off it to left and right. On the left there was a neatly arranged pharmacy, a tiny operating theatre, its space almost completely taken up by the operating table, and a storeroom for linen and dressings. On the other side of the passage were the sleeping quarters for the staff (a male orderly sleeping in the anteroom at the other end of the barge) and a small kitchen where the nurses cooked and ate their meals together. There was also a somewhat ingenious washroom and a water closet that was nothing more than a galvanised metal bucket under a wooden cover with a ring of rubber on the top and known by its nautical name, 'the heads'.

Hedley quickly found that the principles of running a floating hospital were no different from those on dry land, except that everything had to be even neater than usual, and movement around the ward more cautious. The two VADs who were attached to the barge were hardworking and eager to learn, and Madam O'Gorman provided first-rate leadership, organising staffing rosters, ensuring that supplies never ran out and liaising with neighbouring hospitals with regard to patient admissions. A doctor from the Bergues hospital visited the barge twice a day to make a morning and evening round and stayed for longer periods to perform operations. The dirty linen, which in an ordinary hospital could be consigned to some spacious laundry where it would be washed and returned without delay, had to be removed at regular intervals by washerwomen who visited the barge several times a day. The barge's dressing station was a converted furniture pantechnicon, parked in a field at a safe distance from the barge, from where the soiled dressings would be taken away by the orderly and burned in a bonfire. The patients' main meals were brought in from a canteen set up by the Friends' Ambulance Unit in the nearby village, whilst the preparation of the morning coffee and tartine, as well as other drinks throughout the day, were the responsibility of one of the VADs.

Morris's arrival just four days before Christmas 1915 was both a joy and a relief to Hedley, who had been trying, with Madam O'Gorman's help, to act as both day and night sister on the barge. Sister Robinson had come to the end of her contract a few days earlier and had returned to England for a well-earned rest, and Morris was to be her replacement. In a bid to make Christmas on board as festive as possible, staff ingenuity was stretched to the limit, and great was everyone's delight when a Red Cross parcel labelled 'Christmas extras' arrived. The Isle of Wight barge had not been forgotten by the worthy ladies at Red Cross headquarters in London, who that year dispatched a total of 10 500 tins of sweets, a ton

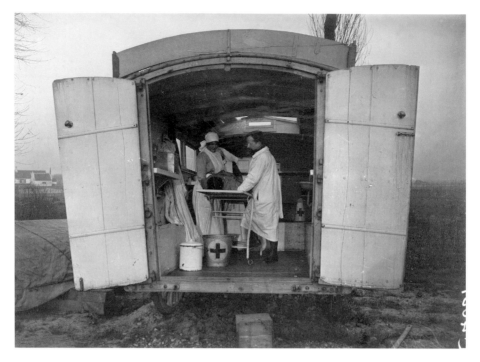

Dressing station for barge

each of Brazil nuts, walnuts, chestnuts and filberts, 2½ tons of almonds, three tons of dried fruit, 10 000 boxes of crackers and 20 000 Christmas cards to hospitals across France.

Although the barge was considered by local hospitals as particularly suitable for the care of longer-term sick and injured, there was also a constant throughput of patients, some of them out-patients, and the Red Cross records for the fortnight ended 19th February 1916 state: 'number of patients treated forty-four; daily average number of new patients ten; operations performed during the period two'. To understand the nature of the various conditions that Hedley and Morris were required to treat, it is necessary to look at the appalling circumstances from which the patients, young and old, had dragged themselves.

* * *

The German War Book, the *vade mecum* of every German officer, stated that when occupying an area 'the civilian inhabitants must be intimidated and made to suffer by every possible means and with no least atom of weak mercy'. In this way it was hoped that the moral atmosphere created in the invaded nation would cause it speedily to sue for peace. Once the German army had entered a town or village, scientific and complete destruction would ensue, and this would be carried out even more thoroughly if the army were forced to retreat. One after another the houses and barns would be set alight, and the larger buildings such as church or town hall blown up by dynamite. If the inhabitants survived the onslaught, and these would of course be women, children and the elderly, since the menfolk had long since gone off to join a regiment or been killed, they would be forced to live packed together in the burnt-out remnants of their homes, often existing in the cellar with just a makeshift roof to shelter them. In these airless conditions and without running water, people soon fell victim to all kinds of disease, tuberculosis being a constant threat, and an almost total disinclination for food very quickly set in. Very often the inhabitants would be driven out of their villages altogether, and waves of them could be seen plodding wearily along the roads of northern France, the lucky few with handcarts to carry their remaining possessions. Many of them died in ditches from hunger and weakness. Not content with destroying all the buildings in the towns and villages through which they passed, the Germans also made a thorough job of destroying all sources of food. Fields would be churned up or set fire to, crops would be destroyed, and machinery smashed. Fruit trees would be deliberately sawn through above the roots, or, where there was no time to finish this task, deeply gashed all round.

This was the landscape from which the patients who found themselves within the whitewashed walls of the Isle of Wight barge had come. Some, particularly the very young and the very old, were suffering simply from malnutrition, exhaustion or exposure. Many had shrapnel wounds from the shelling and dynamiting of their villages. Others had been injured by un-exploded hand-grenades when digging in the fields for food. There were broken bones and head injuries from collapsing beams and walls. In many cases, gangrene had set in where injuries had been left too long untreated, and these would often lead to amputations. Hedley and Morris nursed patients through every sort of disease with the exception of typhoid, these cases being transferred to a typhoid hospital not far away. They were there to offer emotional support where there was so much anguish and grief, and where prolonged strain and long-deferred hope had become unbearable.

* * *

This book does not attempt to be a scientific medical record of the care that nurses were able to give during the First World War, long before the discovery of antibiotics and sophisticated methods of surgery; other books have explored that specialised area. It is enough to say that Hedley and Morris were required to use almost every aspect of their training on a daily basis for the seven months that they spent on the barge. The work was hard, and the shifts long, and their very rare half-days off had to be taken individually, or the barge would be left without a sister in charge.

It was sometimes difficult to occupy the patients who were on the road to recovery, although Madam O'Gorman ensured that there was a constant supply of books sent up from the FAU supply depot. Whenever time allowed, Hedley and Morris would sit and read to the children and teach them English nursery-rhyme songs to entertain the other patients. A flurry of

Barge on the Canal de la Haute Colme

excitement would run through the barge each time there was an official visitor. The orderly would give the linoleum an especially thorough clean, and the VADs would ensure that their 'hospital corners' were particularly neat when making the beds. At the beginning of February the Médecin Chef of the Bergues hospital paid a visit, and there was much holding of breath when, on 1st March, the Principal Matron of the Red Cross in France herself, Nora Fletcher, visited the barge. This august lady pronounced herself satisfied with what she found. There was even a rumour that the Queen of the Belgiums and Prince Leopold might drop in after visiting the Hôpital Elizabeth in the middle of May, but to everyone's relief the royal couple never materialised on the barge. For the staff there were events organised by the FAU, and Hedley and Morris tossed a coin to see who would attend the concert party in the Malo Casino at the beginning of July.

In the middle of July 1916 both Hedley's and Morris's appointments terminated, and they were replaced by two new sisters. The barge was by this time in need of repair, and for a couple of weeks in August the patients were accommodated in tents that had been erected for the purpose on the canal bank nearby. Much in need of a rest, Hedley and Morris returned to their respective families in England to spend the summer recuperating. In September they returned to Brixton and took up the reins again at Loughborough Park, happy to be delivering babies once more and training a new intake of pupil midwives.

Sources

Archives de la Croix Rouge Française, Paris.

Library of the Religious Society of Friends, London.

BANKS, Arthur. *A Military Atlas of the First World War*. Heinemann Educational Books, 1975.

BINYON, Laurence. *For Dauntless France*, Hodder & Stoughton, 1918.

British Red Cross Society, op. cit.

MACDONALD, Lyn. *The Roses of No Man's Land*. Michael Joseph, 1980.

MEABURN, Tatham and JAMES, Miles (eds), op. cit.

MITCHELL, Anne. *Medical Women and the Medical Services of the First World War*, 1978.

PINCHEDEZ, Annette. *Péniches-Ambulance, Péniches-Hôpital*. L'Association des Amis du Musée de la Batellerie, 1999.

War Organisation of the British Red Cross Society & Order of St John of Jerusalem, op. cit.

Chapter 9
Into Battle

If thou faint in the day of adversity, thy strength is small.
Proverbs 24:10

Madam O'Gorman continued to keep in touch with Hedley and Morris and in the middle of January 1917 she reported that the French authorities wanted to take over her barge for military cases. The Belgian civilian patients were to be transferred to other hospitals, and the barge was to await the new arrivals in the middle of March. Rumours were going round of a new French offensive, and Madam O'Gorman was only too well aware of the challenges this development would present. She wrote and asked whether Hedley and Morris had thought of applying to the JWC for a further appointment. The two women discussed the idea and decided that Morris should apply for a second posting to the barge immediately, leaving Hedley to look after the Midwifery Institution in Loughborough Park. If the situation in France had not changed by the autumn, then Hedley would join her.

Morris rejoined the Isle of Wight Barge at the end of April 1917 and found a rather different set of medical conditions to cope with. In place of the boys and old men that had filled the ward previously, the patients were now moustachioed *poilus* suffering from gunshot and shrapnel wounds, gas-infections, a considerable amount of sepsis and bad cases of gas-poisoning. The little operating theatre, which previously had to cope with two or three operations a week, was now rarely idle, and there was a doctor living permanently on the barge. Four weeks after Morris's arrival the barge was moved again to work in attachment to a French evacuation hospital that was receiving wounded soldiers down the line, and now the pace became frantic.

By September the situation on the Western Front was growing worse. The Third Battle of Ypres, which was to culminate in the battle of Passchendaele, was underway, and the Germans had started to use mustard gas for the first time in the war. Hedley decided that it was time once again to leave Loughborough Park and rejoin Morris for her second appointment on the Isle of Wight Barge. On her arrival at the barge, Hedley was struck by the change of pace and atmosphere since the previous year. Horrific injuries were being borne with astonishing courage and good humour, and the sense of camaraderie was palpable. A good night's sleep had become something of the past, and the two Sisters had to resort to catnaps whenever the opportunity arose. The barge was coming under constant shelling now, and on one occasion sustained minor damage while Hedley was assisting with an operation. Such was the need for additional medical support in the area that in January 1918 two French military hospital barges were brought alongside the Isle of Wight Barge, bringing the number of beds to ninety. Madam O'Gorman was given charge of the nursing and general supervision of all three barges, addressing some of her staff in English and some in French.

At the beginning of March, the Principal Matron of the JWC in Boulogne notified Madam O'Gorman that it was time for Hedley and Morris to take home leave again. Since it would be quite impossible for them to be absent from the barge at the same time as one another, it was decided that Hedley would take her fortnight's leave first, and then Morris would take hers immediately afterwards. By the time Hedley returned to France on 20th March, the Germans were making their last bid for the channel ports, and the area was coming under heavy bombardment. Madam O'Gorman and her team were doing their best to keep going in extremely difficult conditions, but a few days after Hedley's return the decision was finally taken to withdraw the barge to a safer location. The Queen Alexandra Hospital had already been forced to evacuate its hospital sheds at Malo-les-Bains to the Château de Wevre in La Petite Synthe on the Bourbourg Canal, so the Isle of Wight barge was moved to a point nearby and handed over to the hospital to be used for treating the French civilian wounded of the Lys Valley. Madam O'Gorman and Hedley were instructed to proceed to the Château de Fontainebleau, 50 km south of Paris, where their services were urgently needed. Morris was to join them there later.

Shortly after leaving the barge, Hedley was sent the following testimonial from the Chief Medical Officer of the Hospital Barge Taskforce. As it is one of the few documents to have survived, I shall quote it in translation in full:

Sister Hedley-Peek, of the English Red Cross, qualified at the Victoria Hospital London, in general service at the hospital barge unit. This nurse displays thorough and professional competence in the exercise of her duties, which she carries out with a remarkably methodical approach, truly exemplary discipline, the greatest conscientiousness and absolute dedication. Her most correct behaviour on the one hand, and her total devotion on the other have gained her the greatest respect among the wounded soldiers, as well as their confidence and gratitude. The courageous attitude of this woman, in the course of the frequent bombardments this area has suffered, has had the happiest influence on the morale of the soldiers under treatment.

* * *

The Château de Fontainebleau was a vast Renaissance-style palace surrounded by extensive park and gardens dating from the middle of the fifteenth century. As soon as war had broken out in 1914 it had been stripped of its sumptuous furniture and wall-hangings and closed to the public. The following year the apartments in the Louis XV wing had been converted into hospital wards for 500 wounded, and further beds were installed in the Pavillon du Tibre in the park. The indoor tennis court, or jeu de paume, had been converted into a centre for mechanotherapy – a new idea from the Nordic countries – and up to 400 patients per day were being treated with a special electrical apparatus that was intended to exercise and strengthen their muscles. Later that year Lord Kitchener was to visit the palace, accompanied by the Minister for Foreign Affairs, Sir Edward Grey, but this was long before Hedley and Morris took up their duties there.

In comparison to the cramped and somewhat primitive conditions on board the barge, Fontainebleau must have felt more like a highly organised ocean liner to Madam O'Gorman, who was now heading a small team of English nurses in an otherwise entirely French hospital. Each of the vast salons and galleries was able to accommodate long rows of beds, and the hospital was equipped with the most modern appliances, X-ray facilities and instruments, not to mention a large team of doctors, surgeons and nurses, as well as numerous orderlies, porters and domestic staff. Hedley and Morris's routine now was largely dictated by the arrival of ambulance convoys, of which there seemed to be a never-ending stream both day and night. Motor vehicles filled with empty stretchers would stand lined up in the courtyard of the Château, and when the message came that a convoy was expected, the ambulances would set off for the railway station,

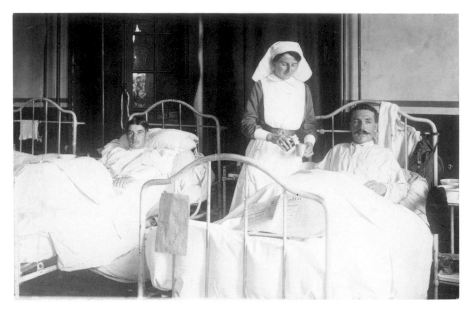

Ward at the Château de Fontainebleau

Hedly, Morris and Madam O'Gorman with English patients at
Château de Fontainebleau

84

where they would exchange their empty stretchers for others bearing the wounded. These would be transported as gently as the roads would allow back to the Château, where they would be briefly examined by a doctor, X-rayed and allocated to a ward, where Sister and her team would be standing ready to receive them and prepare them for any necessary surgery.

During the recuperation period the soldiers were encouraged to move about as much as possible, play cards and receive visitors. As on the barge, fresh air was considered vital to speedy recovery, and on warm dry days, the orderlies would carry or wheel the fitter patients out into the park, where they would sit or lie on chaises longues, sometimes playing a game of boules from their prone position under the huge lime trees. Nurses would often be required to read to the patients or write letters for them, and Hedley and Morris found themselves constantly in demand among the English soldiers who had been brought to Fontainebleau prior to being repatriated.

After the somewhat chaotic routine on the barge, staff rotations were strictly adhered to at Fontainebleau, and for the first time the couple were able to take days off together, a favourite excursion being to the artists' colony nearby at Barbizon. But the lull in the frenzied activity that had characterised the two women's lives for so many months was not to last. They had been nursing at Fontainebleau for only a few weeks when the summer offensives of 1918 began, and the call went out for volunteers to work in the surgical ambulance teams that were accompanying the French armies into battle. Without a moment's hesitation, the intrepid pair signed up.

* * *

Described by Georges Duhamel in 1918 in his book *Civilisation*, as 'the most perfect thing in the line of an ambulance that has been invented … the last word in science; it follows the armies with motors, steam-engines, microscopes, laboratories', these Ambulances Chirurgicales Automobiles (ACAs) were an astonishing piece of ingenuity on the part of their inventor Dr Marcille, who, as well as being a well-known Paris surgeon, was clearly an engineer by nature. Marcille reasoned that a wartime medical service need only apply – on a far larger scale and as close to the battlefield as possible – the same principles as the emergency surgical service offered in peacetime by any top-class Paris hospital, and success would be assured. Paris surgeons had always kept an operating theatre in their hospitals ready for serious accident cases; all they had to do now was replicate those aseptic conditions in a fully mobile operating theatre, along with facilities for preparing the wounded for surgery and arrangements for their recovery afterwards.

Marcille's design for the composition and staffing of the ACAs had undergone several revisions since their first trials in 1915. At one point no fewer than eleven lorries had been required to transport and house the necessary machinery, medical equipment and personnel, and the military were far from happy at seeing so many valuable vehicles immobilised in this way. By the time Hedley and Morris joined ACA No. 7 in May 1918, the Marcille ambulance was being transported in six trailers[1], so that the lorries could be freed up for further duties once the formation had been towed to its new location.

In all there were 43 ACAs – one permanently attached to each army, and the remainder allocated as military manoeuvres required – and the new layout of the ambulances ensured that they could follow the army wherever it went. When advancing, the army would be accompanied by the operating theatre together with one of the canvas wards; the other ward would be left in its original position until all the patients had been evacuated and then move forward to join the rest of the formation. When the army was retreating, one ward would be carried back in advance to make ready for the arrival of the operating theatre and the second ward. Moving the heavy ACA equipment around and erecting the formation in position was a tricky task, and a considerable amount of time was spent looking for a way through the waterlogged terrain and ensuring that wheels did not disappear into ditches. Once in the new location further time was spent consolidating the ground with sleepers and logs before erecting the many canvas wards, storerooms and corridors that made up the formation. Because of this lack of mobility, the ACAs were at great risk of damage or even capture, and

---

[1] (1) Sterilisation trailer divided into three sections: at the back autoclaves and sterilizers for gloves, brushes, bowls etc.; in the centre a steam boiler and a dynamo for providing lighting in operating theatre and wards; and in the front radiography equipment and electric cabling.
(2) Linen trailer with lockers for dressings, instruments and pharmacy.
(3) Laundry trailer that would be installed next to the sterilisation trailer for supply of steam and power.
(4) Central heating trailer that produced warm air and had a mobile kitchen at the back.
(5) Trailer carrying the panels and canvas walls of the hospital wards.
(6) Trailer carrying an emergency generator and a dynamo for lighting and hospital radio.

for this reason were always kept about 20 km behind the front lines with the wounded being transported to them by a fleet of ambulance lorries.

The layout and functioning of the Marcille ACA was specifically designed to accommodate an incessant flow of casualties, with virtually no limit as to number and gravity. After the wounded man had been unloaded from the ambulance lorry that had transported him and others from the battlefront, he would be carried on a stretcher via an office, where his details would be registered, to an area where he would be undressed, washed and warmed up. He would then be wrapped in a warm blanket, X-rayed and, when the time came for him to be taken into theatre, anaesthetised with chloroform using an apparatus known as an Ombredanne. The operating theatre itself was a hive of activity with four surgical teams

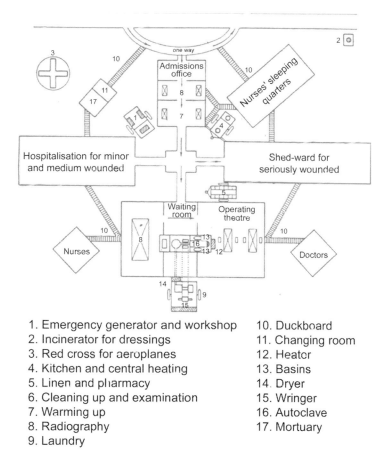

1. Emergency generator and workshop
2. Incinerator for dressings
3. Red cross for aeroplanes
4. Kitchen and central heating
5. Linen and pharmacy
6. Cleaning up and examination
7. Warming up
8. Radiography
9. Laundry
10. Duckboard
11. Changing room
12. Heater
13. Basins
14. Dryer
15. Wringer
16. Autoclave
17. Mortuary

Interior layout of Marcille's mobile surgical ambulance, 1917 working at two operating tables in eight-hour shifts around the clock. With the aim of treating one wounded man per hour per table, the number of operations could reach fifty in a 24-hour period, although in short bursts of intensive military action it was not unknown for all four teams to be working simultaneously with only short breaks for meals. After the operation the wounded man would be taken to one of the wards, where he would be cared for until fit enough to be transported to a permanent hospital further down the line. Marcille's surgical ambulance units enjoyed a truly phenomenal success rate, but it has to be said that this was not solely due to their design. It was well known that only the most highly regarded surgeons were selected to lead each unit in the role of Médecin Chef, and that these doctors gathered around themselves élite teams that guarded their reputations proudly and not a little competitively.

And it was in just such a team, ACA No. 7 led by Médecin Chef Dr Georges Lardennois, that Hedley and Morris found themselves working when in May 1918 General Ludendorff resolved to reclaim the Chemin des Dames Ridge near Soissons that the Germans had lost to the French a year earlier. This 'Third Battle of the Aisne' was the final large-scale German attempt to win the war, and Ludendorff's ferocious artillery bombardment of 4000 guns followed by a gas attack resulted in heavy casualties in the Allied front-line trenches. The Chemin des Dames offensive was followed in rapid succession by the Battles of Château-Thierry, Belleau Wood, and – the last major German offensive of the war – the Second Battle of the Marne, all of them played out in the area between the Vesle and Marne rivers, the very area where Hedley and Morris worked from May to August with ACA No. 7.

The pace and tension of their life in the surgical ambulance unit can only be imagined, but in his history of the medical service in the First World War, Chief Medical Officer A. Mignon includes a description which gives a fair idea. I give it here in translation:

> The main aim was not to lose a moment.… The surgeon, after washing his hands, took his tray of instruments out of the autoclave himself, laid them on a table, put on a robe, apron and gloves and was ready to operate. After use, the instruments were immediately cleaned, put in the boiler and then put ready for the next operation. As soon as the wounded man was taken out, the lino floor would be cleaned with a wet cloth, and the next man brought in. The surgeon would take instrument trays from bottom to top and from

front to back, and when he had taken the last one, six new trays would be put in the autoclave and sterilisation would begin immediately so that the surgeon could do six more operations as soon as he'd finished the first six.

This extraordinary throughput of patients depended entirely on a support team of male and female nurses, VADs, administrators, laundry staff, electrician, carpenter, driver and even blacksmith – all working in finely timed coordination with one another.

After four months of exhausting yet exhilarating work on ACA No. 7, Hedley and Morris were each presented with an official letter from Dr Lardennois in which he commended their 'nursing skills, zeal and devotion'. They were sent back to England for three weeks well-earned rest, Hedley arriving just in time to attend the funeral of her beloved grandfather, Joseph, who had died on 20th August in his ninety-fifth year. When they returned to France they rejoined Madam O'Gorman on the barge at La Petite Synthe and resumed their work caring for the civilian wounded.

* * *

On 11th November 1918 the long-awaited Armistice was declared. Hedley and Morris were aware that they would shortly be eligible for demobilisation, but neither had the least intention of going home just yet. The remaining British wounded soldiers may have been transported back to England by now, but ahead lay the monumental task of repatriating the tens of thousands of British Prisoners of War, many of whom would be extremely sick men, that were being released from camps across Germany. The majority of British POWs were slowly making their way to the ports of Holland and Belgium where they were shipped back to England, but those being held in camps in southern Germany, particularly those too weak for a long journey, were crossing straight into France. Madam O'Gorman applied to the JWC for authorisation to proceed with Hedley and Morris to the German border near Strasbourg, where they would establish a POW reception hospital. The JWC replied that they had received no instructions to this effect, but nothing daunted the three women resolved to undertake the mission in a private capacity – a not at all unusual arrangement during the First World War. Without delay Madam O'Gorman arranged to have the barge moved down the dense network of rivers and canals that criss-cross north-eastern France to the town of Nancy, where it was moored on the Marne-Rhein canal, not far from the German border.

At the time of the Armistice, there were no fewer than 185 Prisoner of War camps scattered across Germany holding approximately 167 000 British prisoners, with a further 10 000 from the dominions and colonies of the British Empire. There were camps for officers and camps for other ranks, factory camps, agricultural camps and general work camps. The worst conditions were to be found in the camps that sent men to work for twelve hours a day in the mines, especially the salt mines where they would develop painful open sores on their arms and legs and where supervisors would beat them if they were deemed to be working too slowly. But common to almost all the camps, and the most insidious and demoralising torment, was the chronic shortage of food. Men were kept day in, day out on little more than starvation rations – maybe a mug of ersatz coffee made from burnt barley or acorns and a thin slice of black bread adulterated with sawdust for breakfast, and soup for lunch made out of the water in which the guards had boiled their own meals with odd pieces of vegetable floating around. Crucial to the men's survival were the food parcels from England, but their arrival had started to break down as the German transportation network crumbled.

Under the terms of the Armistice, Germany was required to release all Prisoners of War immediately and provide them with the necessary transport home, but central authority in Germany had largely broken down by this stage, and in reality the process of repatriation was protracted and confused. In some cases prisoners found that their guards had simply deserted them, leaving them to make their own way out of Germany. Those interned in camps in the west of Germany could simply walk in the direction of friendly forces (if they were strong enough to do so), while others held in camps near the Polish border had to wait for anything up to three months to be brought home. By the end of November fewer than ten per cent had reached England, and even by the beginning of January 1919 at least 14 000 British POWs were still languishing in Germany.

From November to February fleets of ambulances were sent into the interior of Germany to collect those who were very sick, and many of them were to remain in France or Holland for recuperation before continuing their journey home. These were the men that were brought to the barge – men in a pitiful state, often weighing as little as six stone, some walking with the aid of two sticks, their faces gaunt and their eyes staring. The three women had to take enormous care in re-establishing anything approaching a normal diet, as many of the men were suffering from disorders such as dropsy, a potentially fatal illness caused by their appalling diet. Malnutrition had also caused terrible sores, which were invariably infected and needed constant dressing. In their weakened state, several of the men had fallen prey to the influenza epidemic that was sweeping Europe, and many did not survive. One thing all the men had in common, however, was a desperate desire to go home, and Hedley, Morris and Madam O'Gorman did their best to get the men into sufficient shape to manage the journey.

Little by little the flood of men coming over the border began to abate, and the need for medical attention to become less pressing. Madam O'Gorman decided that she could manage the barge with just one trained nurse to help her, and it was decided that Hedley would return home. She made her way to Boulogne, where she was officially demobilised by the Joint War Committee on 20th December 1918, and was able to spend Christmas with her family. Morris remained on the barge a further two months and was demobilised on 14th February 1919.

Sources

Centre Historique des Archives Nationales, Paris.

Archives de la Croix Rouge Française, Paris.

Service Historique de l'Armée de Terre, Château de Vincennes, Paris.

BANKS, Arthur. op. cit.

British Red Cross Society, op. cit.

MACDONALD, Lyn. op. cit.

MIGNON, A., Médecin Inspecteur Générale. *Le Service de Santé pendant la Guerrre 1914–1918*. Masson et Cie, 1926.

MITCHELL, Anne. op. cit.

NUSSBAUM, K. *Map of the Inland Waterways of France*. Imray Laurie Norie & Wilson Ltd, 2001.

VINCENT, A. *Fontainebleau: le palais, la ville, la forêt*. Société d'éditions Artistiques, Paris, 1920.

Chapter 10
Devastation and Deprivation

To be able to leave home, to stay away from it without complaining,
to enter into the lives of foreign peoples is among the freedoms that
distinguish civilisation from provincialism – a freedom upon which
the greatness of great nations has depended since Rome established
her provinces and mariners set out to discover new worlds.

Review of Julian Green's *Memories of Happy Days*

In common with countless other women who had witnessed the horrific
sights of the First World War, experienced the powerful sense of camaraderie, and been forced to draw on all their resources of courage and energy
to play their part, Hedley and Morris found it difficult to adjust to life back
in England. Visions of the shell-torn villages and the hollow-eyed children
who lived there were never far from their minds, and in the summer of 1919
they once again approached the Red Cross to see if they could return to
the devastated areas of northern France and help in the relief work there.
Their application was passed to the French Red Cross, who after the war
had set up a Comité Britannique in London to smooth the path of those in
the UK wishing to help in this way. Shortly afterwards Hedley and Morris
were dispatched to the Comité unit at Reims, where they were to work
under the direction of an Englishwoman with a distinguished nursing
career, Celia du Sautoy. Miss du Sautoy had been matron of a British nursing
unit attached to the French army during the war and was living with her
associate, Lady Hermione Blackwood, the daughter of the famous English
statesman, Lord Dufferin, in an 11th century poorhouse in Reims.

Within a short time of Hedley and Morris's arrival in Reims the unit's
funds were running dangerously low. The main purpose of the Comité had
been to provide direct relief, and now that the money was running out it was
beginning to shut down its operations in preparation to withdraw. The sickness among the people of Reims, and in particular the condition of the
children, crowded as they were into airless cellars and unsanitary ruins, was

Village near Reims 1919

still appalling. The city of Reims held a meeting and offered free quarters, heating, lighting, water and telephones if the British would only leave their nurses behind. The Comité replied that their remaining funds would not even cover the cost of maintaining the staff, let alone the provision of healthcare. But before the Comité could close down its operations in Reims and send Hedley, Morris and the other nurses back to England, two intrepid American women, Anne Morgan and Anne Murray-Dike, stepped into the breach. Somewhat to their surprise Hedley and Morris found themselves working not for a French but for an American organisation.

* * *

Anne Morgan was born in New York in 1873. She was the youngest daughter of the banker, John Pierpoint Morgan, who had left her one of the richest women in the world when he died in 1913. Throughout her life Anne had had a great love for France, making frequent visits there to stay in the Villa Trianon in Versailles, and when war broke out she immediately became involved with the American Fund for the French

Wounded (AFFW) in New York. In 1917 Anne read about the terrible plight of the civilian population in the devastated areas of northern France. Together with her partner, the somewhat mysterious Anne Murray-Dike, and a group of friends, Anne Morgan returned to France and, with General Pétain's support, founded her organisation – the Comité Américain pour les Régions Dévastées de la France, known to all as CARD.

General Pétain installed the group in the ruins of the Château de Blérancourt about seventy-five miles north of Paris and had seven barrack-style wooden buildings constructed in the château grounds to accommodate staff and stores. The official task Pétain gave CARD was 'to bring whatever aid they could to the civilian population of the Département of the Aisne', one of the most devastated areas on the Western Front, placing the organisation under the orders of General Humbert, Commanding Officer of the Third Army. CARD duly adopted a uniform of military jacket and skirt in French Army blue, fixing metal gryphons to the lapels that they had copied from the arms displayed on the château's gateway, and chose as their motto a native American proverb, 'Do Right and Fear No Man'[1].

To begin with the group of American women, who seemed to flout almost every convention of their class and times, were regarded with a fair degree of suspicion. One French officer was more than a little surprised when he entered his office one day to find Anne Morgan perched on the edge of his desk, removing a cigarette from a distinctly masculine-looking cigarette case. But when the French saw how energetic, effective and highly organised CARD was, they were more than happy to work closely with these unusual women, who would sweep all aside with the simple statement '*on est du Comité*'[2].

---

[1] All CARD associates were presented with a medal bearing the Blérancourt gryphon on the face and the motto on the obverse. The medal ribbon was French Army blue – *bleu horizon* – with white stripes. It is reproduced at the end of this book.

[2] A wonderful contemporary description of the two Annes survives in Gaston Hericault's *Terres Assassinées*. Anne Morgan is depicted as 'a tall woman, with a proud air about her, buckled tightly into a blue uniform, her greying curls escaping from under a hat perched at a jaunty angle on her head. What struck me most were her black eyes, sparkling with intelligence, which emphasised the curve of her generous mouth and chin.' Anne Murray-Dike is described as 'tall and svelte, so thin that she could almost be described as diaphanous; her golden red curls, escaping rebelliously from beneath her blue hat, framed an almost emaciated oval face with huge, bright eyes, full of intelligence but also of melancholy! Her thoughtful gaze fixed on you unnervingly and seemed to be searching your soul; then her plump, finely drawn lips opened slightly to form a warm smile that lit up her entire face. But within this fragile exterior there dwelt a strong character and a lively will, which were truly exceptional.'

For the first eighteen months of its existence CARD concentrated its efforts on getting temporary shelter, food, clothing, bedding and basic furniture to the devastated villages in the area, delivering their provisions in a fleet of Ford vans shipped over from America and driven and maintained by a team of women under their chief mechanic, Louise Barney. What was becoming increasingly clear to the women of CARD by the end of the war, however, was that there was an urgent need for medical care in the region, particularly for children. No civilian doctors had so far returned to the area, and the population were relying on the few military doctors who had stayed behind. A fully trained nurse named Mary Breckinridge had by now arrived from America to join the CARD unit in the devastated area around Vic-sur-Aisne. Appalled by the general state of health and malnutrition that she found, Breckinridge persuaded Anne Morgan to let her run a special care programme for children under six and pregnant or nursing mothers, making home visits and working from the Consultation de Nourrissons clinic she set up. So great was the success of the project that Anne Murray-Dike asked Breckinridge to extend it across the whole of the CARD sector, which by now stretched across four cantons of the Aisne Département – 127 communes with a total population of 60 000 people. Breckinridge was clearly going to need a number of additional trained nurses and was surprised to discover that no visiting nurse service existed in France. However, by the end of 1919 she had managed to persuade the matron of the only lay nursing school in France at that time – the Florence Nightingale School attached to the Maison de Santé Protestante at Bordeaux – to send her seven of her newly qualified nurses.

Mary Breckinridge had met Celia du Sautoy and Hermione Blackwood when the Comité Britannique had been stationed at Compiègne, not far from Blérancourt, and decided it was time to pay them a visit in Reims. When she heard about their dilemma and saw the continuing need for nurses in the area, Breckinridge asked Miss du Sautoy to draw up a budget and hurried back to Paris to lay the problem before Miss Morgan and Mrs Murray-Dike. It was agreed that CARD should take over the Reims unit from the Comité Britannique and from now on both the Union Jack and the Stars and Stripes were to be seen flying outside the new headquarters. Breckinridge was given responsibility for the British nurses, who were placed in pairs, Hedley and Morris of course together, in four wooden sheds or 'baraques' donated by the city of Reims. Here they slept and ate, and from here they set out each day on their home visits, being collected by a CARD driver or travelling around by bicycle if no transport was available. Each pair of nurses was allocated to one of four areas of the city – Courcy, St Brice, Chalet and St Nicaise – with a total population of 20 000.

Although France had yet to adopt the idea of the 'infirmière visiteuse', it had an extremely well-developed system for the training of midwives, the course lasting no less than two years and culminating in an examination and diploma. If Hedley and Morris had expected to continue practising as district midwives, they were to be disappointed, since there was no shortage of qualified French midwives working in the area. The midwives were, however, happy to hand over mother and baby to the visiting nurse once the infant was ten days old, since they could appreciate the benefits to the nursing mothers of the extra nutrition provided by CARD. When it was not possible for a woman to be delivered in her home, the French midwives were also happy that the expectant mother be admitted to the American Memorial Hospital – still in its temporary accommodation in the shattered buildings of the 17th century Hospice for Incurables – where she would stay for fourteen days after the delivery, receiving instructions on the future care of her baby and being sent home with a complete layette. This hospital, funded by the American Fund for French Wounded,

Hedley leaving CARD 'baraque' to make a home visit

had good links with CARD, and Hedley and Morris worked closely with the staff there both during and after the mother's admission.

Despite a crop of what were known as 'Armistice babies' in the summer of 1919, the birth rate in France had fallen dramatically as a result of the war, and one of the main preoccupations now was repopulation. Hedley and Morris knew that the battle for each child's life had acquired an additional significance, but they also knew that without adequate nutrition for both children and nursing mothers it would be a losing battle. Many of the children who had remained in the villages under German occupation were two or more years below their age in size and strength, and most were pitifully undernourished. But once again Mary Breckinridge hit on an ingenious idea: goats.

Until the fields of the devastated areas could be ploughed and re-sown and the stock of cows replenished – which was to take some considerable time in war-bankrupt France – goats could provide the much-needed milk for mothers and children. Goats could survive for most of the year on the weeds and brambles that had managed to push their way through the rubble of the ruined towns and villages. Over in the United States people were invited to 'sponsor a goat at 20 dollars apiece', and collections were made for 'beetroot money' to feed them in winter. Wagonloads of goats soon began to arrive from the Pyrenees, and before long they were joined by a fine buck (ensuring future generations of goats in the months and years to come). The buck was given the name 'Ambassador' after American Ambassador Morgenthau who paid a visit to the project.

As might be expected, and despite the valiant efforts of the American Friends, demand for goats vastly outstripped supply, and a strict allocation system had to be applied, a system which on one occasion Hedley and Morris succeeded in subverting. One of the villages for which they were responsible was in urgent need of milk and was not due to receive its allocation of goats for some time to come. Hearing that a wagonload of goats was passing nearby, Hedley and Morris colluded with the local railway worker to shift a set of points. As soon as the train-driver realised that he had taken a wrong turning, he brought the train to a halt, whereupon the doors to the gloomy goat wagon 'somehow' fell ajar, allowing the inquisitive goats to push their way out into the sunshine. It did not take long for the animals to 'disappear' into the village, where they were quickly relieved of their milk.

The children under six needed a considerable degree of feeding and care just to keep them alive, and it was wonderful to see the transformation in them after only a few weeks of four glasses of goat's milk a day. Most of the new mothers were so undernourished that they were quite unable to breast-feed their babies. Hedley and Morris found that once they had poured malted goat's milk or chocolate made with condensed milk supplied by CARD into them, they were able to breast-feed to a certain extent, supplementing with bottles of goat's milk. A good many of the children who had been living in the areas occupied by the German army were riddled with impetigo and eczema, and there were numerous cases of tuberculosis, particularly of the bones, largely due to malnutrition. To add to the misery there were outbreaks of both scarlet fever and diphtheria in the villages in the winter of 1920–1921.

Following a hard winter, the summer of 1921 was one of the hottest on record. There were still virtually no sanitary arrangements in the villages, and disease-carrying mosquitoes were now added to Hedley and Morris's burden. An urgent call went out to CARD to provide mosquito netting, and the mothers, who had been previously unaware of the dangers, were instructed about the importance of using these at all times. Fresh air too seemed to be a novel idea to many of the mothers, who also had to be convinced of the benefits of ventilation, one of the basic principles of the Florence Nightingale school of thought. The local people were soon

A typical home

to say that at night you could always recognise a home where CARD nurses had visited by the number of open windows. Persuading the mothers to expose more than a square centimetre of their children's bodies while out of doors proved to be more of a challenge, and this was particularly frustrating to Hedley and Morris, who believed firmly in the benefits of sunshine to tubercular limbs. When a child was giving particular cause for concern, arrangements were made for her to be dispatched with a label around her neck to Mornex in the Swiss Alps, where a CARD unit was able to provide temporary homes for twenty to thirty children at a time.

One way of ensuring that every child's state of health was being regularly monitored was by twice-yearly medical inspections in schools. To begin with the CARD visiting nurses conducted these themselves, but after the doctors had returned to the devastated towns and villages, they were able to take over with the CARD nurse present to note down any necessary follow-up work. The head-teacher would be warned in advance that an inspection was about to take place, and the class teacher would be ready to line the children up in an orderly fashion. Assisted by the CARD nurse, the doctor would weigh and assess each child and careful notes would be taken on index cards. If the child was significantly underweight, he would become eligible for a 'CRB' midday meal of meat, vegetables and bread. The American Committee for Relief in Belgium and France, known as the CRB, had closed down its own operations in the Spring of 1919 and had a residue of thirteen million francs to dispose of. It was decided that this money should be used to feed schoolchildren in the devastated areas, and every child received a cup of chocolate, made with condensed milk, and a biscuit made of flour, sugar and lard at the close of each school day, the most malnourished also receiving the wholesome midday meal. Building on their relationship with the teachers, Hedley and Morris also ran child-care and hygiene classes which both girls and boys were obliged to attend.

* * *

If life for Hedley and Morris was one of almost unremitting duty and hard work, it was still possible, even in war-torn Reims where there was barely a building left standing, to find a little time for enjoyment and relaxation. There were frequent get-togethers with the other nurses in the Reims team, either in one of their hut-homes or at Celia du Sautoy and Hermione Blackwood's home, where there would sometimes be euphonium concerts or poetry readings. Occasionally there would be large-scale gatherings at CARD headquarters at Blérancourt, and for these they would be collected and driven the fifty or so miles in one of the CARD vans. These get-togethers would last two or three days and were intended as much as a social opportunity as one for professional feedback and training. Strong friendships were forged between many of the women, and one such bond was immediately struck up between Hedley and Morris and a particularly striking woman from Philadelphia named Elisabeth Starr. Starr's brother had joined the British Army in 1915, long before America joined the war, and had died on the Front at Ginchy. Starr had set sail immediately for France, where she drove an ambulance for the French Red Cross and was decorated in 1918 for her services. She was now working as a driver in the CARD motor service.

Back at their quarters in Reims, Hedley and Morris tried to make their hut as homely as possible, with Morris in charge of the cooking. Poor Morris would rack her brains to come up with something a bit different, even trying out an ersatz coffee recipe she had been given which involved boiling up acorns – not a huge success. One Christmas day she was determined to produce something really special and, having dug deep into the back of the store cupboard, proudly produced steaming bowls of porridge

CARD nurses at Reims (Morris left, Elisabeth Starr seated on step, Hedley right)

which the couple ate with great relish. Books at least were always in plentiful supply, as CARD had by now set up its mobile library service with books supplied by the New York Public Library and loaded onto the back of one of their Ford vans. This little library, with its eclectic range of books, was greeted almost as eagerly by a book-starved people as the dispensary, and it certainly forced Hedley and Morris to widen their reading tastes in some curious directions.

* * *

And so life went on for the next couple of years, with Hedley and Morris watching the painfully slow rebuilding of the City of Reims, doing their best to heal the bodies and minds of the people who lived there or who were gradually returning. By 1923 public health services had re-established themselves in the area, and it was clear that CARD operations would soon have to be pulled in under their authority. It was decided to close down the Reims unit, and their activities in the cantons of the Aisne were absorbed by the Association d'Hygiène Sociale de l'Aisne, or AHSA for short. A number of the CARD personnel continued to work with AHSA, including Anne Murray-Dike and Anne Morgan[1]. Anne Morgan received numerous decorations from the French government, including the Croix de Guerre, and was made a Commander of the Légion d'Honneur in 1932. Anne Murray-Dike, who also became a Knight of the Légion d'Honneur, died in 1929 and was buried at Blérancourt, where Anne Morgan had founded a Museum for Franco-American Cooperation[2].

By the time CARD withdrew from Reims in 1923, there was a relatively smooth-running child welfare system operating in that city, and Hedley and Morris began to look further afield to where their services might best be utilised. Although the larger towns in the devastated areas were well on the way to reconstructing their homes and public buildings and re-establishing their essential services, many of the small villages were still, five years after the armistice, in a lamentable state. The area around Verdun still looked very little different to the massive battlefield it had once been, and the people of the villages there were depressed by the challenge of clearing so much rubble and creating even the semblance of a civilised life again. Hedley and Morris decided that this was where they might be

---

[1] The organisation still exists today under the name of L'Association Medico-Sociale Anne Morgan in the Rue Anne Morgan in Soissons.
[2] The museum also still exists.

most needed and made an appointment to see Mademoiselle Chardenot, the Inspector of Hygiene for the Département of the Meuse, based in its Préfecture at Bar-le-Duc. Between the three of them it was decided that Hedley and Morris should set up a mother and baby clinic in the village of Hannonville-sous-les-Côtes, about 20 miles south-east of Verdun, and this could also serve as a centre for people from neighbouring villages.

And there Hedley and Morris lived for almost two years, applying the same theories and methods developed by CARD but without the support of its generous American benefactors. The Préfecture was only able to fund the most essential medical supplies but insisted on paying two modest salaries. Hedley and Morris sent home lurid descriptions of the villages where they were working, accompanied by postcards of the bleakest landscapes imaginable. As they had hoped, these resulted in regular donations from the Kidd and Morris families and many of their friends.

The two women quickly found that a bicycle was not a practical way of visiting homes in the surrounding villages, the roads still being full of potholes and rubble. After much careful study of their finances, coupled with further letters home, the decision was taken to buy a car, this causing great excitement in Hannonville. Hedley and Morris had learnt the rudiments of driving from their friend in the CARD motor service, Elisabeth Starr, and thought they understood a bit about basic mechanics. A trip to the Citroën agent in Bar-le-Duc resulted a few weeks later in a magnificent drop-top Citroën 5 with frogs-eye chrome headlights and large rubber claxon. Hedley fell instantly in love with this vehicle, and Morris had to accept that from now on Hedley would be doing most of the driving.

Sources

Ministère des Affaires Etrangères Archives, Paris.

Musée Nationale de la Coopération Franco-Americaine, Blérancourt, France.

BRECKINRIDGE, Mary. *Wide Neighbourhoods*, University Press of Kentucky.

DIEBOLT, Evelyne & LAURANT, Jean Pierre. *Anne Morgan*, AMSAM, 1990.

Ibid. *Les Femmes dans l'Action Sanitaire, Sociale et Culturelle, 1901–2001*. Assn Femmes et Associations, 2001.

HERICAULT, Gaston. *Terres Assassinées, Devant les dévastations (1914–1933)*. Sirey, 1934.

Chapter 11
Children in the Sun

All is a question of balance and of the wise distribution of our energies between the absorption of beauty and the labour of getting things done.

Anon

By the Spring of 1925 Hedley and Morris knew that it was once again time to move on, although this time the wrench was truly hard. The villagers had by now taken the two demoiselles anglaises to their hearts, and the mothers had come to rely on their help and advice. The mayor of Hannonville organised a reception in the Salle des Fêtes, and this was attended by the Inspector of Hygiene for the Département, who made a speech expressing 'the sincere regret of the community at their departure and her abundant thanks to the two women for their devoted service'. On 25th April, amid many tears, the couple packed up the Citroën and set off for a three week driving holiday through France to St Jean-de-Luz, where Morris hoped to catch up with some childhood friends. Hedley kept a precise log each day of the route taken, sights visited and kilometres covered[1] and even recorded an enforced stop in Nevers for Morris to have a tooth extracted.

Over the years most of the women who had been attached to CARD had gradually drifted back to America and England, where they presumably married – or perhaps remained single – and got on with their lives. Mary Breckinridge, impressed by the English nurse midwife model she had encountered in Hedley and Morris, moved to London to train at the General Lying-In Hospital and went back to America to found the renowned Frontier Nursing Service of Kentucky. But some of the women simply found it impossible to go back to the life of genteel boredom that would await them in their native countries and believed that their wish to live among other women was more likely to be accepted in France with its more liberal attitudes.

---

[1] Something that she was to do throughout her driving days.

Elisabeth Starr and Dorothea (Dolly) Watts were two such women. Elisabeth came from a wealthy Quaker family in Philadelphia, and when CARD was disbanded she and Dolly decided to make their home permanently in France, settling on Provence as the ideal place to live. In 1921 they bought the abandoned summer home of some local monks, the Castello san Peyre, which stood largely in ruins looking down a hillside of olive groves and across to the hilltop village of Opio, near Grasse. For the first couple of years the two women lived quietly together, filling their time by supervising the building work and clearing the collapsed walls and dead olive trees to create a garden. But the years spent working for CARD had left their mark, and they could not fail to notice that there seemed to be little provision for the many crippled children in the area. Elisabeth got together a fund-raising committee and set about looking for a suitable location for a hospital for children suffering from bone disease. Not far away on the hillside of Les Gibous she found an old olive press, which could be bought for next to nothing and could easily be converted into a house, and above it the perfect spot to build a small hospital. By the summer of 1925 a simple but modern hospital, L'Hôpital St Christophe, was being constructed. All that was needed now was qualified staff to run it, and a letter was soon on its way to Hedley and Morris, begging them to move to Provence and run the little hospital. Elisabeth's request was successful.

* * *

Hedley and Morris spent the summer months of 1925 with their respective families back in England, Hedley staying in Blackheath with Eileen and Arthur who by now had three children – Hedley, Meriel and Eldred. Her youngest sister, Beryl, who was making a career in the art of Grecian dance and mime made popular by Isadora Duncan, had also married and had a son, John. Hedley soon became a favourite aunt, not least because of the generosity and thoughtfulness of the presents she produced each time she visited. On the morning after her arrival, the children would come into her room and be told to look in her trunk, where they would each find a present. Young Eldred was disappointed one year to be told that this time there was no present in the trunk; instead he was taken into Lewisham, where he was bought a wonderful steam ship that burned metholated spirit pellets and puffed out real steam.

Hearing that St Christophe would not be ready for patients until the following Spring, Hedley and Morris set off from Southampton at the end of October to do a grand five month tour of Italy before taking up their duties. Travelling via Algiers and Genoa, they arrived in Florence, where there was an emotional reunion with Hedley's cousin Noel, who by now had married a wealthy American named Billy Sheldon and was living in the Palazzo Pitti. In the Museo di Storia Naturale in Florence they were fascinated by the wax models of the human form – both inside and out – that had been made by two men in the 18th century, and enchanted by the old priest 'with clean nails – a most unusual occurrence' who took them round the Chiesa di Ognissanti and showed them the robe worn by St Francis. After taking delivery of a brand new Citroën 5, they saw the New Year in at Pompeii, went on a 22-mile walk up the valley of the Alcantara, saw the altar in Syracuse where St Paul was said to have preached and had to jump off the road in Rome as Mussolini's car swept away from his lunch at the Excelsior Hotel. On 12th April 1926 Hedley and Morris drove into France via Menton and arrived in Opio, where, the driving log records:

> … we found Watts waiting for us in the sweetest little house imaginable surrounded by glorious views of the mountains stretching away on every side.

* * *

The hillside, which ran from east to west not far inland from the coast and only a short drive up from Nice and Antibes, was truly idyllic. At the foot of the hillside the land was blessed with natural irrigation, and cornfields stretched in every direction. The hillside itself had been largely terraced, no-one could remember how long ago or by whom, to create olive groves, and these yielded the main cash crop, along with olive oil produced in the numerous olive presses dotted around. Oranges grew in abundance, and vineyards produced a rather rough, though perfectly drinkable, rosé wine. But what struck Hedley and Morris most of all as they arrived that Spring was the spectacle of the flowering plants and shrubs; there were flowers everywhere, and it was easy to understand why Grasse, only 12 miles away, had been the centre of the perfume industry in France since the 16th century. Throughout the year the local people would gather the mimosa, blossom from the orange trees, violets, lavender and roses and take them to Fragonard, or one of the other great perfume houses in Grasse, who would press them in wax to release their essence.

This then would be mixed amid great secrecy by a 'nose' to create perfume or sent on as a perfume base to a famous manufacturer such as Chanel.

The part of the hillside where Hedley and Morris were to make their home was known as Les Gibous (some said because the hills there resembled hunch-backed gnomes) and looked across to the hilltop villages of Opio and Châteauneuf. Opio, the commune to which they would belong, was tiny, but Châteauneuf-de-Grasse, to give it its full title, boasted a population of over 800 people and a bus service to Grasse. Its mayor, Jean Foucard, was the biggest olive oil producer in the area, and there were no fewer than four commercial wine producers. Of particular interest to Hedley were the two garages, run by Mr Humann and Mr Monselesan, and there was even a dressmaker, Mme Bovis, who was married to one of the winegrowers, Frédéric.

After settling into their new home whose name, L'Oustalet, was the Provençale word for 'small house', Hedley and Morris were anxious to inspect the hospital in which they would be working. What they found were a couple of small two-storey buildings standing about 40 feet apart with a single-storey building connecting the two. This lower building, which was to be the ward of the hospital, was set back about ten feet, to allow for a spacious terrace which ran the full length of the ward and faced due south. On entering the ward, they saw twelve white-painted iron beds, complete with sides that could be drawn up and ends that could be raised, and these had been placed six for girls and six for boys on either side of a panel that ran, not quite full height, down the middle of the ward. In the buildings at either end of the ward were an office, a dispensary and a bedroom for the sister on night duty, and upstairs there was accommodation for domestic staff. Hedley and Morris were delighted with what they found and were full of enthusiasm when they were invited to dinner that evening by Starr and Watts. Two days after their arrival Hedley noted in her driving log that 'St Christophe became pregnant'.

* * *

The relatively high incidence of bone disease among the children of rural France in the 1920s could be put down to a number of factors, principal among them of course tuberculosis, for which there was still no inoculation or curative medication. Peasant families tended to be large, ten children not being an uncommon number, and many of these families had either lost their breadwinner in the Great War or had him returned to them in no fit state to work ever again. This did not mean, however, that he could not help to produce yet more children. Mothers were left to provide as best they could for their children, most of whom were severely malnourished, and the standard of hygiene in many of the homes left much to be desired. In common with the families in the devastated areas of northern France, these women would clothe their children from neck to ankles in whatever ragged clothing they could find, leaving not one inch of their bodies exposed to the sunshine, even in the summer. These conditions were a perfect breeding ground for tuberculosis, particularly of the bone. In addition to being threatened by TB, children were not supervised in the careful way they are today, and accidents were common. If the family could not afford to consult a doctor, broken bones would be left to heal just as they were and very often infection would set in. Where a child was admitted to hospital, the shortage of beds meant that he was usually sent home before the cure was complete, often with a limb in a plaster cast that would be allowed to become filthy and infected. Such children, so the patrons of the new hospital believed, grew up to become handicapped adults and a needless burden on society.

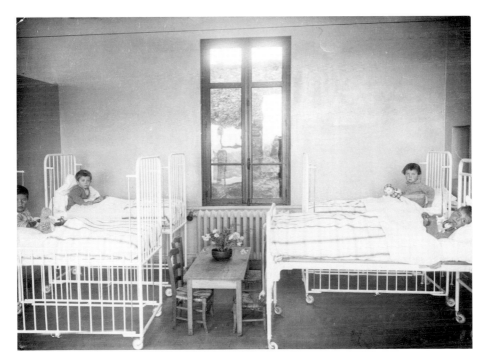

St Christophe interior

109

The treatment provided by Hedley and Morris's clinic could not have represented a greater contrast in the lives of these pathetic little individuals, being based on three simple principles: the very best nutrition, sunshine and immobilisation. There was an absolute commitment that no child would be discharged until completely cured, even if that meant staying at St Christophe for several years. Before being admitted, patients had to produce a medical certificate stating that they were not suffering from any of the usual childhood illnesses, and far away from the dust of the roads and infections of their own homes, high up on the hillside, there was no risk of further disease. Parents were allowed to visit their children once a week on Sundays, and brothers and sisters under the age of fifteen were not allowed to visit at all. Patient referrals usually came from Dr Lenoël, a well-known orthopaedic specialist based in Nice, who also agreed to act as honorary surgeon, re-setting bones or, on rare occasions, performing amputations. A local GP, Dr Reboul, was appointed the official physician to the hospital and visited regularly.

Elisabeth Starr had identified a very real need, and it was not long before the twelve beds at St Christophe were filled with six girls and six boys, exactly as planned. The age range was four (one four-year-old had never been able to walk) to fourteen, although this limit was ignored on more than one occasion. As far as nationality is concerned, the 1931 census shows a strong Italian contingent, this part of the country having been annexed by France relatively recently, and there was even one Russian child.

If sunshine was to be the principal healer of these diseased bones, Elisabeth could not have chosen a more perfect location, since the hillside on which St Christophe was built faced due south and basked in sunshine for most of the day and a good deal of the year. Unless it was raining or judged to be too cold, the children's beds would be pushed out onto the terrace every morning and left there until the evening. The bed-covers would be removed, as would the children's chemises, and there they would lie, completely naked apart from the plaster casts that most of them wore, a tiny modesty garment and a cotton sunhat made by Morris from an array of brightly coloured fabrics. Where complete immobility was required, the child would be attached by a cotton harness to the bed to prevent too much movement. The children who were on the road to recovery were also obliged to remain outside all day and spent their time playing almost naked with their bed-ridden friends or in the gardens beyond.

So profound was Hedley and Morris's belief in the 'purification' brought to their patients by so much fresh air that they soon decided that the

Hedley with patients on the terrace with Châteauneuf in the distance

children should be left out on the balcony all through the night whenever possible. Special canopies were constructed that could be pulled over the top half of the beds, but the bottom half would often be quite damp with dew by the morning. This new idea caused a certain amount of alarm among the parents when they got to hear of it, and some of the children were not too happy either when lizards ran over their beds in the night. Although Hedley and Morris allowed these more timid children to resume sleeping indoors, as a rule they enforced this rather extreme practice.

As far as nutrition was concerned, many of the children had never eaten so much wholesome food in their lives, and when the local people heard that the majority of the St Christophe children were being treated free of charge, they were quick to offer whatever produce they could. Milk was of course an important part of the diet, and this would be carried up the hill every morning by young Louis Tomatis, whose father kept a small herd of cows down in the valley. Another neighbour was Honoré Foucard, who had a large orange orchard nearby. In Spring he would gather the blossom to send to the perfume factories in Grasse, but later in the year he would send basketfuls of fruit to St Christophe, including the bitter variety. These Hedley and Morris would turn into a curious confection called 'marmalade', which the somewhat suspicious children soon got used to eating on their morning tartine. Other donations of food included rabbit, much shot at by the local peasantry, and a weekly consignment of vegetables from an English couple named Griswold who had come to settle in the area. All contributions were gratefully received by the Italian cook, Luisa Loccio, who gave devoted service for many years to St Christophe and lived on the premises.

One of the greatest challenges presented by such a long-term cure as was offered at St Christophe was how to keep the children entertained, not to mention educated. The Committee put out a call for volunteers and before long it was possible to create a rota of women, both expatriate and French, who would spend time playing games with the children or teaching them songs and handicrafts. Overall responsibility for the children's education was given to Nicole Vincens, an unmarried woman who lived in nearby Malbosc with her adopted son Augustin. Nicole was to become a lifelong friend of Hedley and Morris and was one of the few Protestants in the area, worshipping with them at the 'Temple Protestant' in Grasse. The Swiss pastor there would come up to St Christophe once a week and tell the children bible stories, illustrating them with wonderful drawings on large sheets of paper. An English friend, Miss Johnson, who lived with her father in a villa nearby, was particularly good at telling the children stories, sometimes from books and sometimes out of her head, and a local author, Maria Guizol, taught the children to read and write. One of the older girls passed her *Certificat d'Études Primaires* shortly after leaving the hospital. As she could not read when she was admitted, she received almost her entire education at St Christophe.

Because of its idyllic location, there was no shortage of young men and women volunteering to come out from England for a few months, either as nursing staff or to amuse the children. One of these was Morris's nephew, Bryan Preston, with whom one little patient, Lucette Argaud, fell madly in love (he was later to lose a leg in the war), and another was Eileen's dashing teenage son, Hedley. Female relations were required to help with the nursing, apart from Morris's sister Edith, who was a frequent visitor but not required to work very much as she had always been considered 'frail'. It would be best at this point to let one of Hedley and Morris's patients, Juliette Dallo, tell her own story of her stay at St Christophe:

> I was born in 1922. When I was one year old my father took my mother and me into Nice in his horse and cart. The horse shied and fell over and the cart turned over too. My mother and I fell out and my mother crushed me underneath her. At first no-one thought I was hurt, but by the time I was two years old they knew something was wrong with me. My leg had been forced up into my hip and grown crooked and the whole side of my body was badly affected. My parents took me to see Dr Lenoël in Nice and he said my only hope was to go to St Christophe. I was there for four years and I

finally learnt to walk when I was six. Miss Peek never got angry with us, she just explained calmly until we saw the sense of it. Miss Morris used to blush when the dentist came to visit. My parents didn't have to pay a penny for my treatment. They came to see me as often as they could and brought my friend with them.[1]

Hedley and Morris quickly became an institution in themselves among the local population, who christened them affectionately 'la Grosse et la Grande'. People were generally somewhat in awe of Hedley, who tended to peer down her rather Roman nose at them from a great height and who knew exactly what was what. Although her French was by now fluent, she insisted on pronouncing it with an entirely English accent, unlike Morris who had learnt the language from birth and spoke like a native. Morris they found more approachable, and the children certainly knew which of the two Sisters to go to for favours or the occasional cuddle. Regardless of the temperature, the two women insisted at all times on wearing the full nursing uniform that they had brought with them from England. This uniform, which proved to be a real novelty to patients and visitors alike, consisted of long pale blue dress with separate white collar, full-length starched white apron and square white nurse's veil, and white stockings and shoes beneath. Strict duty rotas were kept at all times, and whoever was on night duty, which changed once a fortnight, slept in the little room just off the children's ward.

With its high ratio of staff to children and the additional costs of food, drugs, dressings, clothes and laundry, St Christophe was not a cheap place to run, despite the fact that Hedley and Morris themselves refused to take a salary. Cash flow was the cause of constant anxiety and greatly exercised the Committee that Elisabeth had set up under the chairmanship of a Mrs McNeill. However, the Riviera was awash – particularly in the summer – with the glitterati of Europe, and the list of patrons that the Committee managed to accumulate makes impressive reading. Consuela Balsan, the ex-Duchess of Marlborough, is there, as is La Comtesse Gautier-Vignal, an American living near Nice. Princesse Ghika, an American lady who had married a Romanian Prince, was persuaded to part with her money, and so was the Princesse Torre et Tasso, who lived in a large

---

[1] Mme Dallo was eighty when I met her. She married the little friend her parents brought to visit her in the hospital and together they had five children and numerous grand-children. She showed me one of her most treasured possessions – a photograph of Queen Elizabeth II as a small girl.

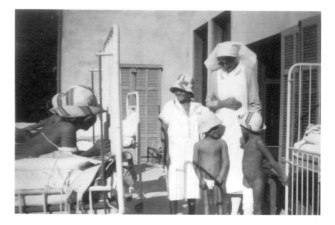

Hedley with patients (Adele del Giorgio standing left)

'domaine' in nearby Magagnosc. Princess Gennaro de Bourbon was even persuaded to join the Committee. Add to these the Baronesses Knut-Bonde and Ramsay, the Comtesse de Labry, and numerous other titled ladies, and you have just a glimpse of the total list of patronesses.

Of male patrons there was only one, HRH the Duke of Connaught, third son of Queen Victoria. On the death of his Duchess and with his health failing, this distinguished gentleman had been ordered by his doctors to spend his winters on the Riviera. Possessed of great good looks and charm, he soon became the most popular royal personage on the Côte and was particularly appreciated by the French for the way he became involved with the local community. His Royal Highness was happy to become the Patron of the Hôpital St Christophe, who were not, however, expecting him to pay a visit. The best description of that historic event has been provided by Adele Bertugli, who as Adele del Giorgio, was a patient of twelve at the time:

> One day there was great excitement. Lots of ladies came all in their best dresses. We weren't told what was happening in case we got over-excited or behaved badly. A very fine man came with his retinue, it was the Duke of Connaught, one of Queen Victoria's sons. Miss Peek and Miss Morris had to curtsey to him. He walked around but didn't say much.

In addition to cash donations, both from local benefactors and from friends and relations in England, St Christophe also relied on the multitude of fund-raising activities that were held by the expatriate community on the Riviera. Bridge teas, jumble sales and theatricals in aid of St Christophe became regular events, the Cannes Amateur Dramatic Club donated a total of Fr.4000 from its takings one season, and the Cannes Casino threw a Gala Dinner. There was a constant flow of gifts in kind, with Princesse Gennaro de Bourbon's working party providing chemises, night-jackets and bibs. One of the original members of Elisabeth's committee, Mrs Carr, had made herself responsible for providing the whole of the hospital linen, no mean feat considering that the children wore out twice the number of sheets as normal because of their plaster casts.

But despite all this, the question of funding remained problematic, particularly at a time of world depression. In 1932 the Committee made a special appeal for funds to avoid having to reduce the number of beds or even close the hospital altogether, and in 1934 two boys had to be sent home in the early convalescent stage for the first time in the history of the hospital so that their beds could be given to paying patients. In her medical report for that year, Hedley comments stridently:

> This we *hope* will never again be necessary, as it is very important
> to keep the children till the cure is really completed, especially in
> those cases where the child returns to a poor home, and the mother
> is often out at work.

But someone was watching over the hospital, perhaps St Christophe who carried so many children over the river, and the number of beds never had to be reduced, nor the hospital forced to close.

* * *

But life was not unremitting toil for Hedley and Morris; with so many willing helpers, some of them with a basic knowledge of nursing, it was not difficult for the two women to take the occasional day off together at last. Usually with a couple of local friends or visitors from England, they would pile into the Citroën and drive off with the roof down to picnic in the surrounding countryside or swim on their favourite beach at St Honorat, a little island off Cannes. There was a trained nurse named Meg Parsons living in the area, and she was happy to take over the running of St Christophe for a few weeks each summer so that Hedley and Morris could take time off either to return to their families in England or to go on one of their famous driving and walking holidays in the Alps.

These holidays, of which a careful log was kept, were meticulously planned in the weeks beforehand and covered vast distances and immense altitudes, often putting the Citroën under considerable strain. However, Hedley's approach to her beloved car was no different to her approach to nursing, and the log is full of references to regular greasing and oiling, the cleaning of plugs and the filling up of accumulators. Punctures seemed to be accepted as par for the course, and Hedley spent a good deal of time changing wheels, invariably on the edge of some precipice. The only major incident recorded was a collision half-way up the valley to Adelboden in Switzerland. The police who were called measured just about everything and took copious notes, but two days later Hedley was able to come to some arrangement, noting in her log:

> In the morning interviewed a member of the Interlaken police in his charming house plus his wife, baby girl, dolls and teddy bears. A most friendly affair.

The range of cols, peaks and passes that the little car was required to negotiate is breathtaking, as are the descriptions of the climbs the two women, armed with knapsack and alpenstock, completed on foot. All over the Italian, Swiss and Austrian mountains they travelled. Closer to home they explored the French Alps, where they would sometimes visit Starr in the little Bergerie she had rented high up in the mountains. As well as driving through the most enchanting countryside and marching up countless mountain paths to gaze at sublime panoramas, the two women often included in their tour a visit to some favourite city such as Vienna, Budapest, Florence or Venice. Here they would visit every art gallery, church, concert or opera they could fit into the time available. Only very rarely are there references in the log to 'feeling lazy' and only once to 'feeling seedy', and it is clear that not a moment was to be wasted. Sometimes it happened that the city they were visiting had a children's hospital that was of particular interest to Hedley and Morris, and then they would make arrangements in advance and be given a guided tour.

* * *

After so many years of driving and car maintenance, it is not hard to imagine Hedley's indignation when a representative from the Ministry of Transport climbed up the hill to St Christophe one day with the news that

Hedley (in blue), Morris (with Gauloise) and friends on the Promenade des Anglais, Nice

she and Morris had to take a driving test. The conscientious young official was deaf to Hedley's protests that, as she and Morris had been driving for fifteen years, they should be exempt. Leaving Morris to look after the children and with extreme ill-will, Hedley climbed into the Citroën along with the intrepid official and set off along the narrow, winding road between the olive groves. All seemed to go well until Hedley was asked to stop the car and reverse around a corner, to which she retorted that in the whole time she had been driving she had never once driven backwards and had no intention of starting to do so now[1]. On returning to St Christophe, Hedley discovered that she had nevertheless passed the test. Not wanting to waste any more valuable nursing time, she suggested to the young man that if she drove him to the station, he might like to issue her colleague with a driving license too, assuring him that Miss Morris drove quite as well as she did. The thought of having to test two such terrifying Englishwomen in one day was clearly more than the young man could cope with, so he agreed readily and shot off back to Nice.

* * *

Throughout the 1920s and 30s, while Hedley and Morris were busy running St Christophe, the hillside around them was becoming so popular with the English that it was re-christened by the local people *La Colline des Anglaises*. One notable arrival on the hillside during the 1930s was Lord Anglesey and his family, the Pagets. Lord Anglesey[2] himself became a frequent visitor, and eventually acquired a ruined château that he set about renovating. One of his elderly relations, Amy Paget, settled permanently in the neighbourhood and was later reputed to have refused to leave her home when war broke out, greeting the Germans at her gate wrapped in a Union Jack. Polly Cotton, known to all as 'Pauls', was another member of the Anglesey family who came to live on the hillside and became a close friend of Elisabeth Starr. There were departures too; Dolly Watts took everyone rather by surprise by getting married and going off to live in the

---

[1] She never did learn to reverse.

[2] He was very charming and had a bit of a reputation with the ladies. In 1937 Hedley's young and very beautiful niece, Meriel, was to travel back alone from Provence after a stay at St Christophe. Her mother suggested to Hedley that Lord Anglesey, who was travelling back at the same time, might escort her. 'Oh no, Ei-Ei,' Hedley replied, 'I don't think that would be at all suitable.'

Hedley, Morris and friends. 'That's Tanneron over there'.

Villa Malcontenta in Venice, where she was later visited by Hedley and Morris on one of their tours.

Another woman who joined the hillside in the 1930s was Winifred Fortescue, whose seven books on life in France – written in the name of Lady Fortescue – became widely read in England[1]. Winifred had been an actress before she married Sir John Fortescue, a man considerably older than herself who had been knighted for his work as King's Librarian and Archivist at Windsor Castle. Due to Sir John's ill health, and also for financial reasons, the couple decided in 1931 to move to the Riviera, making their home just outside Grasse in a house whose renovation Winifred wrote about in *Perfume from Provence*. Upon her husband's death two years later, Winifred moved into a smaller house half-way between Elisabeth's Castello and St Christophe and christened it 'Fort Escu'. From that time onward she was to become a very close friend of Elisabeth and is buried near her in the cemetery at Opio.

This then was the expatriate community with whom Hedley and Morris lived side by side, although always somewhat on the outer edge. Now and then they would be invited to participate in one of the social events, and now and then, when they had time, they would accept the invitation. They were extremely fond of Starr, who had proved her metal to them during and after the war, but had less time for Winifred Fortescue, whom they regarded as 'a bit of a snob' – maybe they were just a little bit jealous of her relationship with Elisabeth. Grateful as they were for the philanthropy of these wealthy people, they saw themselves as set apart from them by the simple fact that they were professionals who had a job to do.

What Hedley and Morris most enjoyed at the end of the day was to sit quietly together and read, very often aloud to one another. Early on they had become members of the Times Book Club, and had enormous fun poring over the catalogue together before sending their monthly order to London. These orders would always include birthday and Christmas presents to be sent direct to relations in England, so that Hedley and Morris became known to their young nephews and nieces as the aunt who always sends a book. Obliged by financial constraints to be cautious and economical in all other areas, they were entirely profligate as far as reading material was concerned, which they considered as vital to survival

---

[1] *Perfume from Provence*; *There's Rosemary, there's Rue*, autobiography 1939; *Sunset House*; *Mountain Madness*; *Trampled Lilies*, story of Provence during WW2; *Beauty for Ashes*; and *Laughter in Provence*.

as food. Perhaps remembering the dogs her young stepmother had bred when she was only fifteen, Hedley had acquired a Pekinese named Yahtzi, who would sit on her lap while she read, Morris reading in a chair opposite with a glass of Pastis in her hand and a Gauloise hanging out of her mouth. And therein lies what was probably the only real bone of contention between Hedley and Morris that anyone can ever remember ... Morris's smoking.

Morris had always smoked, and Hedley had always hated it. Hedley would devise all sorts of ingenious strategies to help her give up; Morris would try them for a few days and then start to smoke again. Hedley tried removing all the ashtrays from the house, but Morris simply found herself a little tin with a lid in which to tap her ash, and this she carried around with her for the rest of her life. Even at the Front, so she told one of her little patients who enquired, when her hands were so purple and numb with cold that she could no longer use them, she could still lift a cigarette to her mouth. Morris was never going to give up her Gauloises, and Hedley was never going to stop trying to persuade her to do so.

Sources

Archive départementale des Alpes Maritimes, Nice, France.

FORTESCUE, Lady Winifred. *Perfume from Provence*. Black Swan, 1935.

Chapter 12
Return to the Front

*If you find your former activities impossible, you must not be passively
resigned to that but find other activities that are possible.*
Ethel Smythe in a broadcast on her 80th birthday

In September 1939 the unthinkable happened, and Europe was once again
at war. In 1914 the people of Châteauneuf and Opio had cheered their
eager menfolk on their way as they marched off to war, convinced that
they would beat the Bosch and be home in time to bring in the harvest.
This time nobody cheered. The 141st Regiment of the Marseilles infantry
was immediately mobilised and stationed in the area with their canteen
in Châteauneuf, and the men were billeted with families throughout the
neighbourhood. To begin with it seemed that the French Army was well
equipped to withstand the threat of an invading force, particularly one
from Italy as would be likely, but as news came in of the capitulation of
the Belgian Army and the retreat of the British Expeditionary Force from
Dunkirk, confidence started to wane. It was not long after the government
had fled to Bordeaux that Maréchal Pétain told the nation that their best
hope was to ask for an armistice.

Although most of the Englishmen of an age to join the forces had
hurried back home immediately war broke out, the fate of the remaining
English residents in the area grew more and more uncertain as it became
clear that France was nearing capitulation. If the Italians decided to occupy
the Riviera, they would almost certainly intern British subjects, and the
Vice-Consul in Nice was asking his Embassy – which had also moved to
Bordeaux – for urgent instructions. Information came through that all
British subjects were to leave France immediately by two coal boats, which
had just unloaded their cargo at Marseilles and had been requisitioned
for the purpose. People were asked to pass the word around to everyone
they could think of and then be on the quay at Cannes by eight o'clock
the following morning with one piece of hand-luggage, a blanket and

three days' provisions. People who chose not to avail themselves of this opportunity would be left to fend for themselves.

Over the previous weeks and months Hedley and Morris had been trying hard to ignore what was going on around them and continue to nurse the twelve sick children in their care, so when word reached them of the evacuation of British subjects, they were dreadfully torn as to what was the right thing to do. As she had so often done before when faced with a conundrum, Hedley went out into the garden to think things over and, to Morris's surprise, came back into the house shortly afterwards to announce with complete certainty that they must go. She later confided in Morris that while in the garden she had come face to face with her mother, who had told her they must leave. Morris immediately set about packing her things.

There was an urgent conference with Nicole, where it was decided that three of the children whose cure was virtually complete could be sent home, and two very sick children would be transferred to the hospital at Grasse. The faithful Nicole insisted that she would be able to cope with the remaining seven patients, assisted by an ex-patient with a tubercular hip and a woman who would come for an hour or two each day to cook. Not knowing what was to become of L'Oustalet, the little house where Hedley and Morris lived, Nicole said that she would bury all the silver and other valuables in the garden to await their return. The beloved Citroën was locked away in the garage that had been built for it further down the lane.

Hedley and Morris had no idea when they would be able to return to St Christophe, nor what state they would find their home in when they did. They were resigned to leaving behind furniture, books and other possessions, but Hedley knew that she could not possibly leave her diaries behind, nor could she carry them with her. She built a large bonfire in the garden and tossed the record of her life, year by year, into the flames. That evening the two women walked to the Castello to say goodbye to Starr who, being an American citizen, was not compelled to leave and who certainly had no intention of doing so.

* * *

The next morning, after saying goodbye to the children, who could not understand why Miss Peek and Miss Morris were obliged to abandon them, and bidding tearful farewells to Nicole and the rest of the staff at St Christophe, the two women made their way to Cannes. A large crowd had already gathered on the quay by the time they arrived, and throughout the day the number of people grew until there were some thirteen hundred in all. Looking at the two coal boats, the Saltersgate and the Ashcrest, that were moored in the harbour, it seemed impossible that so many people could go on board, let alone make the journey back to England. There were people of all ages and classes; large numbers of elderly people who had retired to the Riviera because the cheaper living costs enabled them to continue the life of gentility they had once enjoyed in England; people of delicate health whose doctors had recommended a milder climate; butlers, chauffeurs and governesses and a surprising number of people involved in commerce and trade. Invalids had been brought, some of them on stretchers, from the English hospital, Sunnybank, in Cannes but many of these had to be sent back as it would be impossible to care for them properly on board. Despite the chaos that reigned on the quayside, the French were determined not to waive the usual customs regulations, and no-one was allowed to go on board until their small amount of luggage had been inspected and marked with chalk. One elderly woman died of the heat before ever boarding her boat.

Having passed through customs, Hedley and Morris were directed towards the Saltersgate, which was to take five hundred of the refugees, the Ashcrest taking eight hundred. The crew had spent a couple of days trying to clean the ship, but the iron deck was still covered with a thick layer of coal dust, as were the holds below that were to provide the living quarters for the rest of the voyage and which were reached via hatches and down ladders. It took all day to board all the passengers, the British Vice-Consul among them, but by the evening the two ships were able to set off together on the first leg of their journey. Having arrived the following morning in Marseilles, but forbidden to land, they were told that they would have to wait for the rest of the day to join a French convoy bound for Oran in Algeria, a voyage of five days.

Conditions on board were dirty, cramped and extremely airless below decks. Water was carefully rationed to supply sufficient drinking water for the voyage, and there was virtually none available for people to wash either themselves or their clothes. Lavatory provision had been designed for a crew of thirty-eight, not five hundred. Although people had been instructed to bring their own food with them, not everyone had done so, and no-one was to know that the voyage was to last so long. After three days everyone found themselves standing in the same queue as the unfortunate refugees who had not brought food with them; all now received their rather inadequate rations from the ship's stores. A good deal of the day seemed to be spent lining up under the hot sun, standing on the even hotter iron deck, and it was not long before the ship's stores too began to run short, with meals being reduced finally to a small bit of bully beef and a few biscuits.

But despite the appalling conditions, there was a good supply of stoicism and humour, and true to form it did not take the British long to bring some semblance of order to what would otherwise have been a chaotic situation. Wardens were appointed for each hatch to ensure that the hold was kept reasonably clean and that nobody smoked below deck. Hedley and Morris put themselves in charge of issuing lavatory paper, having succeeded in persuading those who had brought the precious commodity with them that it was in their interests to hand it over. They were also called upon frequently for medical advice and support, although they were relieved to discover that there were other medically trained people on board.

By the time they reached Oran, where they were to await instructions from Gibraltar, the Captain of the Saltersgate had decided that his vessel was really most unsuitable for the number of passengers, all of whom were exhausted and some of the elderly in very poor shape indeed. Everybody hoped to be able to go ashore and then be transferred to a more suitable ship for the voyage back to England, but these hopes were not long-lived. News had reached Algeria that day that France had capitulated, and the Algerian authorities were expecting to be told to hold the ship and intern the refugees. With official negotiations getting nowhere, the Captain got through to Gibraltar on his own wireless and was told to load up with as much food as he could and set sail immediately. The boat joined a French convoy that was leaving Oran that night bound for Gibraltar, where everyone expected to go ashore and find a meal and a hot bath in one of the hotels.

Once again it looked as though their hopes were to be dashed. At Gibraltar a naval officer came on board to announce that no-one was to be allowed on shore and that they must all continue to England in the boats they were in. The Captain and the Vice-Consul persuaded the officer to allow them ashore to put their case before the authorities, and this resulted in the sick, the children, and those over seventy being taken off the boat, leaving just 280 to continue the voyage to England. The boat stayed in Gibraltar for three days, with passengers being allowed ashore for a couple of hours only in batches of fifty. Hedley and Morris managed to buy a few cans of pilchards and the inevitable bully beef, and Morris was able to stock up her supply of Gauloises cigarettes. Work was done on the boat to create more lavatories, and further life rafts were added, since these too had only been intended for thirty-eight people.

After three days, the boat set sail for England, this time in an English convoy escorted by a destroyer and a sloop. There was more space now on the boat, but it did not take long before everyone was filthy again. It was this dirt, more than the lack of food or sleep or even the danger from the constant U-boats that were sighted, that proved to be the greatest destroyer of morale and sanity. Four people suffered complete mental breakdowns during the voyage[1].

* * *

When Hedley and Morris arrived in Liverpool, they were wearing the same clothes they had worn when they left Cannes twenty days earlier. Their first thought, everyone's first thought, was to find a hotel where they could have a long bath and a good night's sleep. The following day they took the train to London along with several of their shipboard companions and then each went on to rejoin their families, Morris to stay with her sister, Ella, who lived in some considerable comfort near Cirencester, and Hedley to stay with Eileen and Arthur, who were by now living in a large house in Oxshott, Surrey. Their three children were all involved in the war effort, Hedley serving with the Chindits in Burma, Eldred an officer in the Royal Navy and Meriel living at home and training as a Red Cross nurse in nearby Leatherhead.

To Hedley and Morris it was of course unthinkable that they would sit out the war in the tranquility of the English countryside. Just as they had done twenty-five years earlier, the two women met up in London and presented themselves at the headquarters of the Joint War Committee that had once again been created out of the British Red Cross Society and the Order of St John of Jerusalem. There Hedley and Morris declared themselves ready for any type of nursing work at home or abroad, on condition that they could be deployed together. Having taken down details of the extraordinary range of their nursing experience and searched through her dossier of positions vacant, the Red Cross Director of Personnel announced that there was a post available as Matron at a Forces' convalescent home in Surrey, but no second vacancy at the same establishment. Hedley and Morris discussed the situation and came up

---

[1] A fellow passenger on the Saltersgate was Somerset Maugham. I have drawn, with permission, on his book *Strictly Personal* for this section of the story.

with a solution: Hedley would take the position of Matron, and Morris would work unpaid as her assistant. The personnel director could see no objection to this idea, so once again Hedley and Morris donned the uniform of Red Cross nurses and, with their First World War ribbons pinned to their aprons, set off for Brookhurst Grange, where the Commandant of the home, Mrs Nesta Flack, awaited them.

Brookhurst Grange was a large house built in 1890 on the lower slopes of Holmbury Hill in the village of Ewhurst, not far from Cranleigh. The house was owned but not lived in by Sir Kenneth Lee, who had made his name and his money in the cotton mills of Lancashire and was now head of the Broadcasting Division of the Ministry of Information. Sir Kenneth lived nearby, and when war broke out he was approached by his neighbour in Holmbury House, the Hon. Arthur Ernest Guinness, second son of the 1st Earl of Iveagh, with the request that he lease Brookhurst to him. Arthur's wife, Marie, was President of the Ewhurst branch of St John Ambulance and she thought the property would make an excellent convalescent home for members of the Forces recovering from war wounds. Sir Kenneth was happy to comply with this request, and Marie Guinness and her team set about making the necessary adaptations to the house, her husband offering to speed up the men's recovery with 'a bottle of the black stuff' at every meal.

During the four years that they worked at Brookhurst Grange, and assisted by local members of St John Ambulance, Hedley and Morris cared for a total of 3240 patients. Among these were 32 Australians, seven Newfoundlanders, two Norwegian sailors and seven Italians classed as 'cooperating prisoners'. The patients had already received treatment previously in a military hospital and had been transferred to Brookhurst either because they were not yet considered fit to return to active service or, in some cases, to relieve pressure on beds in the hospitals. Whatever the patient's physical condition, the two women understood their task to be – as always – the fullest rehabilitation possible of body, mind and spirit. Unless they were bedridden, the men were encouraged to take plenty of exercise in the 24-acre grounds or to walk a little further up the hill and make use of the Holmbury House swimming pool which Arthur Guinness had kindly made available to them.

Although Ewhurst was located deep in rural Surrey, it nevertheless suffered its fair share of enemy action. Being too heavily laden to climb over the hills, German bombers crossing the Channel from France would aim for the 'Dorking Gap' on their way to London and sometimes off-loaded their unspent incendiary bombs there on the way home. In 1944, V1 flying bombs – commonly known as doodlebugs – aimed at London from their launch pad in the Pas de Calais, would often fall short of their target in the Surrey countryside. Appropriate air-raid drills and procedures were also part of the daily routine at Brookhurst.

Men from Brookhurst Grange soon became a familiar sight in the pub, church and post-office of Ewhurst in their bright blue suits, white shirts, red ties and regimental hats, and the residents did their best to make them welcome. Local members of St John Ambulance formed nursing rotas under Hedley's direction, and St John cadets helped at the weekends, waiting at table, taking meals to the bedridden and washing up afterwards. Every Friday evening during the winter months there would be a lecture given by a local resident, topics ranging from the Indian Jungle, to Conjuring, to Hollywood, to Jerusalem. The Ewhurst Parish Magazine, which reported on the lectures, voiced the suspicion that some members of the audience might have prolonged their convalescence so as not to miss any of them. There were also concerts and fund-raising events –

Patients and staff at Brookhurst Grange; Hedley standing between Arthur and Marie Guinness

usually opened by Mrs Guinness – such as the Victory Garden Show in October 1942.

Numerous letters survive from grateful patients. 'It was such a joy to see the men being treated like humans', says one. 'Until my recent experience, I had no idea that such facilities were available to "other ranks" of the forces', says another. Yet another pays tribute to Hedley's 'fine work as the power behind the scenes, ensuring as it does smooth working and physical and mental comfort for the patients'. The wife of one of the patients felt sure that 'the atmosphere of pleasantness and kindness amongst the staff and the men was responsible for the recovery to health of the patients in the minimum of time'. Another patient was convinced that the secret of his rapid recovery was the Guinness.

* * *

In the summer of 1944 it was clear that all was not well with Morris. She had been suffering from abdominal pain for some time but had persistently refused to seek medical attention, saying it was all 'a fuss about nothing'. When she was finally persuaded to consult a doctor, cancer of the bowel was diagnosed. It was decided that Morris should go and stay with her family in Cirencester, where she could have her operation and be cared for afterwards by her sister, Ella. Although the operation was deemed a success, Morris was severely weakened by it, and there was no question of her returning to Brookhurst Grange. Hedley visited her in Cirencester as often as wartime travel restrictions would allow. Much of her remaining free time she spent visiting her sister, Eileen, in nearby Oxshott, or tramping around the Surrey countryside with her niece Meriel. The two of them would set out early to see how much of the county they could cover by bus and on foot. At the end of the day the weary Meriel would return to Brookhurst to sleep on the sitting-room floor – according to her aunt the only safe place to be when the doodlebugs were overhead.

Sources

Ewhurst History Society.

Cranleigh History Society. *Waste not, Want not! Surrey childhood.* 2003.

Ewhurst Parish Magazine, Nov 1941, Jan 1942.

MAUGHAM, W. Somerset. *Strictly Personal*, Doubleday, 1941.

Chapter 13
Back to Provence

What if I live no more those kingly days?
Their night sleeps with me still.
I dream my feet upon the starry ways
My heart rests in the hills.
I may not grudge the little left undone
I hold the heights, I keep the dreams I won.

Geoffrey Winthrop Young

The following year peace was declared, and the convalescent home at Brookhurst Grange was wound up. Hedley was anxious to return to Provence as quickly as possible since Nicole had written to her about the appalling conditions there, with 80% of the children suffering from rickets, skin diseases and gastric trouble due to malnutrition. Morris was still not fit enough to make the journey to France, and so it was agreed that Hedley would go on ahead, with Morris joining her when she felt stronger.

The Provence that Hedley returned to in 1945 was a very different place to the one she had left so suddenly five years earlier. The people who greeted her were pale and emaciated and dressed in the most pathetic rags, their feet poking out of shoes that were only just holding together. Transport into the area, whether by lorry or train, had almost totally ceased, and as a result there was a severe shortage of food, people not being able to survive on the local produce of wine, oil and perfume. Many of the old faces had disappeared, but the person whose absence was the most poignant for Hedley on her return to Opio was Elisabeth Starr.

Being an American citizen, Elisabeth had been able to stay in Provence when the mass exodus took place in 1940. With most of her friends departed, and seemingly oblivious to the dangers, she threw herself into working for the Resistance with an almost total disregard for own health and well-being. A known harbourer of Jews, she was at one point confined to her property, where she was under observation by the Gestapo. In 1943 she died from what appeared to be a combination of exhaustion and starvation and was buried in the little cemetery at Opio. The local people had brought stones to the grave from her beloved Castello and planted white carnations in the form of a victory V, Elisabeth's favourite gesture of defiance.

One face that was not absent, however, even if it was tired and a little haggard, was that of Nicole. Somewhat apprehensively Hedley made her way up to the house, which had been used as German officers' quarters after Hitler had ordered troops into unoccupied France in November 1942. To her enormous relief, the house was in impeccable order – nothing had been defaced, damaged or removed. Leaving her bags in the house, Hedley was led by Nicole up the garden to the hospital, which was in a lamentable state. The roots of cypress trees had cracked the main drains, and a previously unsuspected subsoil of clay had sunk to the point that gaping holes had appeared under the building, causing cracks in the walls and ceilings inside. Nicole had done her best to maintain the hospital but, without funds to carry out the necessary running repairs, she had been unable to prevent what were now clearly major problems.

But help was at hand in the person of Winifred Fortescue. Along with her compatriots, Winifred had been obliged to return home in 1940 and had spent the war years living in Lewes in East Sussex, working as an intrepid spokesman for an association of English lovers of France known as the Association des Volontaires Français. For the first three years, she had managed to keep in touch with Elisabeth and had been devastated in 1943 to hear of her death. Before falling ill, Elisabeth had served on a relief committee for the children of Provence, working with the Quakers and acting as the representative of the American Red Cross. On the day that France was liberated, a moment that Elisabeth had so longed for and worked so hard in the Resistance to achieve, Winifred decided to set up an appeal in her memory and continue Elisabeth's work for children. For the next few months she organised the collection and sorting of garments, shoes, soap, toys and medical supplies, until these eventually filled 108 packing cases. The first English woman to return to Provence, Winifred was able to distribute this desperately needed relief to the children in time for the Christmas of 1945, earning herself the enormous gratitude and affection of the local people and the name 'Maman Noël'[1].

In addition to donations in kind, Winifred had also raised funds in England for what she dreamed would be a permanent relief centre for maimed and crippled children along the lines of the Chailey Heritage

---

[1] This is engraved on her headstone in the cemetery at Opio where she lies not far from Elisabeth Starr.

Hospital near Lewes, with which she had become involved. Having failed to find a more suitable location elsewhere, Winifred decided to spend the money she had raised repairing St Christophe which, she hoped, could then be extended to include additional wings, a small operating theatre and workshops to teach disabled children a trade. Although Winifred's dream of a French Chailey was never to be realised, St Christophe was repaired and repainted and had a completely new drainage system installed by the time Morris rejoined Hedley in the Spring of 1946.

To begin with the regime at St Christophe continued very much as before, although the programme of nutrition was severely complicated by the very harsh system of rationing that remained in place in Provence for some time to come. Three years of drought and the cutting off of the water supply had been fatal for everyone's vegetables. Bread, when you could get it, was a mixture of maize and ground olive kernels, and a white substance made from nuts called *Végétaline* had to serve as a substitute for fat. There was no meat or fish at all, but at least the small quantity of milk that was produced by local cows was reserved for children, so that St Christophe was still able to lay hands on a limited supply of milk.

Little by little life returned to normal on the hillside, and the indomitable Provençale spirit was able to assert itself once more. People were busy again pressing olives, treading grapes and gathering flowers, children were making their First Communion, and couples were getting married. In her book *Beauty for Ashes* Lady Fortescue gives a colourful account of a golden wedding celebration, and this includes a memorable description of Hedley, who had also been invited to the party. The happy couple's son-in-law, Louis, is flirting shamelessly with the female guests when there was more dancing:

> ... and this time Louis bowed low before the English directress of Elisabeth's little hospital. Known and respected by all for the selfless devotion with which she and her friend and partner have tended the sick and crippled children – for love – for so many years, she was sitting bolt upright, clad in a clean striped cotton dress, not a hair out of place, her hands folded in her lap, her clear blue eyes dancing with amusement at the antics of the old people who were again dancing vigorously. A perfect type of good, straight Englishwoman who would prefer to die rather than shirk her duty or swerve one hair's breadth from her standard of justice, truth and integrity. Louis stood before her, a cheeky light in his eyes and his arms held

out questioningly. To my immense surprise – and delight – she went into them, and in a moment was whirling around in a kind of mad polka. I was secretly jealous. She is two or three years my senior – and she was dancing with the rest. I adore dancing, but no one had asked me to dance.

If only life could have gone on just like this, but St Christophe's days were numbered. Such were the exorbitant prices in post-war France that the repair of the hospital alone had all but exhausted the money Lady Fortescue had collected back in England. The hospital's previous source of funding had disappeared with the departure from the Riviera of the wealthy ex-patriate community during the war, and there was no way now of covering even the most basic running expenses. With great reluctance and with enormous sadness, it was decided in 1947 to hand the hospital over to the Rayon du Soleil, a French charity that rescued homeless children and found adoptive parents for them. For a couple of years St Christophe was used as an orphanage and, with the smaller cots that were used, was able to house up to thirty children at a time.

* * *

Hedley was now sixty-three and Morris, not as fit as she used to be, sixty-six. Hedley knew that it was time to draw stumps and retire from professional life. Where better to spend their retirement years than precisely where they were – in their beloved Provence? Nicole Vincens had recently bought a plot of land in a new housing development in the nearby village of Magagnosc, halfway between Châteauneuf and Grasse; she had had a house built there, intending it for her adopted son, Augustin, whose carpenter's shop was just nearby, but Augustin had other ideas, and the house, La Gittaz, remained empty. Nicole was more than happy to let the house at a peppercorn rent to Hedley and Morris, enabling them to sell their hillside home and live off the proceeds. Because of its prime position, L'Oustalet was quickly sold to the retiring British Ambassador to Rome, Sir Noel Charles, who pulled down the crumbling hospital and replaced it with a swimming pool. The little buildings at each end that had served as the hospital pharmacy and office were retained and converted into guest accommodation.

Although she was to live there for the next fifteen years, Hedley never really took to La Gittaz, referring to it always as an 'ugly little house'. The

Hedley and Morris on the balcony at La Gittaz

balcony where they had taken their meals at L'Oustalet had had an uninter-
rupted view down the hillside, across the valley and up to the hilltop town
of Châteauneuf a couple of miles away. The balcony of La Gittaz, on the
other hand, looked down over a small patch of rocky land that had yet to
be transformed into a garden onto a tangle of trees and rooftops. But with
the help of their maid, Lucienne, Hedley and Morris were able to turn the
empty house into a comfortable home and, together with their odd-job
man Jean-Paul, managed to create a little garden out of the scrub, complete
with English lawn. The acquisition of a new Pekinese, Gobi, also helped
Hedley and Morris to settle into their new home.

The English community had largely drifted back to the French Riviera
by now, and with their lives no longer dominated by a demanding nursing
routine, Hedley and Morris soon found themselves caught up in the
whirl of expatriate activity that had quickly reinstated itself. Almost every
day people would go calling, or were called upon, for afternoon tea or
evening drinks or to play bridge. The pair became regular worshippers at
the English church of St John in Grasse[1], which had been opened by

[1] Now known as the Chapelle Anglaise or sometimes the Chapelle Victoria because of the
three stained-glass windows donated by the Queen.

Queen Victoria in 1891 and since 1945 had been used by both the French Reformed and Anglican churches. There were also trips to the English Theatre in Cannes, and visits to sick friends in the English hospital, Sunnybank, which had survived the war. And when all this socialising became too much for them, the two women would just sit quietly together, Morris reading the Manchester Guardian with her 'wretched Gauloise' hanging out of her mouth and Gobi on her lap, and Hedley reading the latest book that had arrived from Hatchards in Piccadilly.

French friends remained an important part of Hedley and Morris's life, especially Nicole Vincens and other former members of the St Christophe staff. With so many of their ex-patients still living in the neighbourhood, Hedley and Morris did not see why the tradition of the St Christophe Easter reunion should not be transferred to La Gittaz. Seemingly unaware that many of their patients were now adults, they would organise the usual Easter-egg hunt in the garden with a magnificent English tea afterwards.

Not able to bear the heat of the Riviera in the summer, the couple would set off in the Citroën every July for a two month expedition, one year for a return to England, and every alternate year for a walking holiday in Italy, Switzerland or Austria. As before there were visits to Noel in the Palazzo Pitti and to Watts in Venice. It did not take long before La Gittaz became a favourite holiday destination for many of Hedley and Morris's relations, although the limited space available meant that couples had to be accommodated in separate bedrooms. Visitors had also to accept that they would be totally organised by Hedley, who would become quite short with them if they were not prepared to follow her advice on which beach to bathe from or when to have meals. No-one was allowed to drive the beloved car apart from her nephew Hedley, although he came dangerously close to losing this privilege when he suggested to his aunt that she might like to enhance the performance of the flipper indicators by fitting them with light bulbs. Their grander friends and relations preferred to stay in the Carlton Hotel in Cannes, and then Hedley and Morris would join them for the day, taking the hotel lift down to the beach, where they would be brought iced drinks by the waiters. Hedley was notorious for sweeping aside anyone who had been thoughtless enough to sit on the boardwalk that led down to the water's edge with an 'Out of the way, out of the way.'

And so the years rolled by, punctuated by the annual rituals of marmalade-making in January, the February outing to the Tanneron hills to see the mimosa, the patient reunion at Easter, the major summer expedition and the pilgrimage to lay flowers on Starr's grave at Opio on

31st October each year. By 1962, however, it became clear to both Hedley and Morris that their days in France were numbered. Morris was 80, Hedley three years younger, and they knew that once their health began to deteriorate, they would be quite unable to afford the cost of healthcare in France. Having spent the greater part of their working lives caring for the wounded, sick and disabled of their adopted country, the irony of the situation cannot have escaped them, but the two women faced this new challenge with their accustomed mix of practicality and optimism. After almost half a

Hedley in the Alps

century spent living abroad, they would return to live in England permanently.

After some preliminary research, and armed with a list of addresses, the couple returned to London at the end of June to carry out a reconnoitre of suitable places to live, staying a few days in each. The accommodation offered by Miss Bowers was conveniently situated in Eaton Square, but the rooms were too small. Miss Burns's house, Otterden Place near Faversham, was indeed beautiful but was deemed to be too exposed and too isolated. A further possibility in Hailsham was rejected as 'distinctly second class'. On a cold and wet August day they arrived at the Whitwell Hatch Residential Hotel just outside Haslemere and came down to tea to find fires burning in both lounge and dining-room. Morris approved; the decision was made.

The couple returned to Magagnosc and little by little prepared for their final departure the following March. La Gittaz, which still belonged to Nicole Vincens, was placed in the hands of an English estate agent, and from time to time prospective tenants, most of whom Morris declared to be quite unsuitable, came to view the property. The house was eventually let to an English couple, Mr & Mrs Gamble, for a period of two years.

The furniture that had been loaned to the orphanage at St Christophe some fifteen years earlier was now donated permanently to the Rayon de Soleil organisation which had run it. In his letter of thanks the Founder-Director, Monsieur Fort, assures his Chères Demoiselles:

It is with enormous regret that we see you leaving France after many years of such devoted service to our young compatriots.

During the winter months various friends arrived at La Gittaz and departed with pieces of furniture that Hedley and Morris would not have space for in their new home in England. Morris was able to sell much of her silver in Cannes, and the considerable library of books, with the exception of a few treasures, was distributed among members of the English-speaking community. A week before the couple left France, fourteen ex-patients were invited for a farewell tea of champagne and cake and were asked to choose a memento to take home with them. The Mairie in Grasse was good enough to issue an export permit for the remaining furniture to be returned to England (whence it had come in the first place), and this was crated up and sent on ahead by rail. The Salvation Army was happy to take the electric stove.

Morris on last day at La Gittaz

On Tuesday 26th March 1963 Hedley and Morris mowed the grass, ate their lunch and at 2 o'clock locked the front door of La Gittaz for the last time. They took five days driving up to Le Touquet where, without a reservation, they loaded the car onto the Silver City Air Ferry bound for Lydd in Kent. They were never to return to France again.

Source
FORTESCUE, Lady Winifred. *Beauty for Ashes*. William Blackwood & Sons, 1948.

Chapter 14
Final Years

As the sun sets but never dies,
Even so shall the sun of my life set
But I shall not die.
Immortality, Rabinchanath Tagore

The Whitwell Hatch Residential Hotel, a rambling Edwardian structure not unlike Hedley's childhood home, stood on top of a hill outside Haslemere in Surrey. The house, which looked south towards Black Down, the highest point in Sussex, was set in substantial grounds with many lawns, shrubberies and brick paths, but the pièce de resistance, as far as Hedley was concerned, was the walled garden that enclosed a well-maintained croquet lawn. The hotel was owned by a Captain and Mrs Daniels, who kept their residents happy by providing them with proper respect for their privacy and dignity and plenty of prunes and junket. Hedley and Morris were to find the other residents genteel, elderly and mostly congenial. The rooms that the couple had managed to secure just a few doors apart on the south side of the house were sufficiently spacious to accommodate the few pieces of furniture and treasured books they had brought back from France, so that lunch guests could be invited upstairs for a preprandial sherry or Pastis without embarrassment.

With the Citroën to whisk them around the countryside, the first few months after Hedley and Morris's return felt little different from their previous biennial visits to England, and they soon became a well-known sight with their open roof, French number plates and steering wheel on the 'wrong side'. But before long the French number plates had to be exchanged for English ones, and shortly afterwards Hedley was notified that she was required to take a driving test. Much incensed (and probably nervous lest she be asked once more to reverse around a corner), Hedley presented herself at the test centre in Chichester, only to fail the eyesight test before even pulling the ignition lever. A nice man from the Haslemere

Morris in her room at Whitwell Hatch Hotel

School of Motoring was subsequently persuaded to take her round the test course (with her spectacles appropriately adjusted), but shortly afterwards Hedley failed the driving test for the second time. Her driving days were over.

As a keen mountain walker, living on top of a hill was quite to Hedley's liking. Even beyond her ninetieth birthday she insisted on walking the mile-and-a-half into Haslemere and when negotiating the steep homeward journey she would apply her golden rule – that one should start off at a pace one knew one could maintain right to the top, no matter how slow that might be. The town itself provided many attractions, with its well-stocked public library and the Haslemere Educational Museum. There were plenty of cultural events there, and Hedley and Morris made regular trips to the Festival Theatre in Chichester. Very occasionally Hedley would take the train up to London without Morris to see a play or visit an exhibition; a highlight of 1972 was the Tutankhamun exhibition at the British Museum, at which a most indignant Hedley was pushed around in a wheelchair by her great-niece[1] who, she was well aware, was using her aged aunt principally as a means of jumping the three-hour queue.

Croquet was once again a consuming passion and a most serious business. Everyone invited to lunch in the summer was challenged to a

---

[1] The author.

Hedley aged 88 with her great-great niece, Anna (author's daughter),
at Whitwell Hatch Hotel

game afterwards, and anyone labouring under the illusion that it was merely a question of banging coloured balls through metal hoops and having a bit of fun was quickly disabused of such notions. When she could not persuade Morris to join her in a game, Hedley would commandeer another Whitwell Hatch resident, an elderly colonel proving himself the most accommodating. She was also a faithful supporter of the Haslemere Cricket Club, whose grounds lay conveniently nearby. Another favourite pastime was Canasta, and here she found an enthusiastic partner in Morris, whose eccentric interpretation of the rules Hedley found somewhat trying.

Hedley would often remark that it was 'important to know the trends.' To the end of her life she was genuinely excited by advances in medicine and the sciences, and it was entirely characteristic of her that the last picture she stuck into her photograph album was a newspaper-cutting of the earth photographed from the moon in 1969. She held strong opinions about people of advanced years, regarding bungalows as a most pernicious invention that discouraged elderly people from using their legs, and did not believe that anyone should live beyond the age of 90. As far as this latter theory was concerned, however, Morris decided that for once Hedley should not have it all her own way.

In April 1973 Morris celebrated her 91st birthday despite having slipped and broken her hip a year earlier. A few months later she fell again, and this time it was clear that she was not going to recover. Hedley made daily trips to Haslemere hospital to sit with Morris and knew that she would soon be separated from her forever. In the middle of the night of 28th June, Morris died peacefully in her sleep. Breaking the habit of a lifetime not to reveal her emotions in her diary, Hedley's entry for that day reads:

Morris died at 2.30 am. So lonely.

Despite having lived with her for 63 years, Hedley was not allowed to identify Morris's body, since she was not a relation, and Morris's nephew Michael had to be sent for to carry out this formality. At the funeral some days later Hedley laid flowers on Morris's grave with a card on which she quoted from Lord Dunsany's First World War poem, *Songs from an Evil Wood*:

> *When will she come again,*
> *Though for one second only?*
> *She whom we love is gone*
> *And the whole world is lonely.*

* * *

After Morris's death the light seemed to have gone out of Hedley and she suddenly began to look old. Although she continued to invite friends and relations to lunch at Whitwell Hatch, making her irritation abundantly clear if they were less than punctual, and was happy to go and stay with them in their homes, it was as though she was waiting for something. She had a firm belief in the after-life, which she regarded as an exciting adventure, and would happily admit that she was looking forward to meeting up again with her mother and sisters – and of course Morris. The winter of 1977 was a hard one, and the fires at Whitwell Hatch were kept constantly burning in the hearth. Hedley's only outing now was to feed the birds, and despite feeling distinctly 'seedy' she did this for the last time on 14th February 1978. Three days later, at the age of 92, Clare Hedley-Peek died.